WORLD
HISTORY

Volume II

WORLD HISTORY

Volume II
The Age of Exploration to the Nuclear Age

BY JOANNE SUTER

A Pacemaker® Book

FEARON/JANUS/QUERCUS
Belmont, California

Simon & Schuster Supplementary Education Group

Project editor: Stephen Feinstein
Designer: Terry McGrath
Cartographers: Jean Ann Carroll, Sharon Johnson

Photo credits:
THE BETTMANN ARCHIVE: illustrations and photographs
on title page and pages 5, 6, 8, 13–18, 21, 22, 24, 26, 27, 29,
33–41, 47, 48, 50, 51, 56, 59, 60, 64, 67, 69, 74–77, 84, 86, 92–94,
97, 99, 100, 104–106, 108, 112–116, 118–120, 123–125, 127, 130,
131, 133–138, 142, 146, 148, 150, 152, 153, 157–160, 162,
169–174, 177, 178, 180, 181, 183, 184.

ISBN 0–8224–7476–X

Library of Congress Catalog Card Number: 88–80704
Printed in the United States of America.

2. 10 9 8 7 6 5 4 3
PA

Contents

Introduction

History is all about change, and this book tells of many changes.

During the Age of Exploration, there was a big change in the way people pictured their world. People came to understand the true shape of our planet. They realized that the Earth is round, not flat. Explorers set out on long ocean voyages. They discovered a huge body of land where they had thought there was only ocean. North and South America took their role in the story of the world.

Another word for change is revolution. Ideas of freedom, democracy, and independence swept across the world. This led people in many countries to revolt. In both the Old World and the New World, people rose up and demanded freedom.

Revolutions in industry and in agriculture changed the way people lived. Discoveries and inventions often helped people lead better lives. But sometimes changes made life harder. For example, industrialization made life in England better for many people. But life became harder for the people who had to work in the factories.

Out of the age of exploration grew an age of imperialism. Imperialism is the quest for more land and more power. Large nations set out to rule smaller ones. Weaker lands were forced to accept foreign cultures and ideas. A strong Europe tried to set up colonies all over the globe.

Many countries tried to fight this. People wanted to control their own lands and lives. The spirit of nationalism led people to unite under their own flags.

And, as histories must, this book talks about wars. World Wars I and II were the worst wars of all time. This book tells how they happened and how they changed nations. Some nations became weaker; others found new power.

And what about today's world? We are still in the process of revolution. Day after day there are changes in science, in technology, and in relations between countries. And there are still many difficult problems that need to be solved.

To us, ancient times may seem very simple and uncomplicated. But were they? The Sumerians in the city of Ur, for example, were kept very busy. They worried about feeding their people and making barren lands yield crops. They struggled to defend themselves against their enemies. And they also had to face the dangers of nature, like floods. They invented new ways to get from one place to another more quickly. They set up governments and made laws. They tried to explain their own existence through religion. And they educated their children. They celebrated life through art and writing.

Are we really so different today?

Chapter 1

Explorers, Traders, and Settlers: An Expanding World

Words to Know

conquistadors Spanish conquerors

insurance a guarantee that a person or company will be paid money to cover losses

interest money paid for the use of other people's money

investments money lent to businesses in order to get even more money back

piracy the robbing of ships on the ocean

Puritans members of a 16th- or 17th-century English group of Protestants; they wanted to make the Church of England simpler and stricter

shareholders people who own one or more parts (shares) of a business

stock shares in a business

trappers people who trap wild animals for their furs

Look for the answers as you read:

1. How did Columbus happen to discover the New World?

2. Who were the Spanish conquistadors? What lands did they claim?

3. How did the Spaniards treat the Indians?

4. How did slave trade develop?

5. Which Europeans settled the east coast of North America?

6. What European countries were the trading powers of the 1600s?

7. How did trade with the New World affect European life?

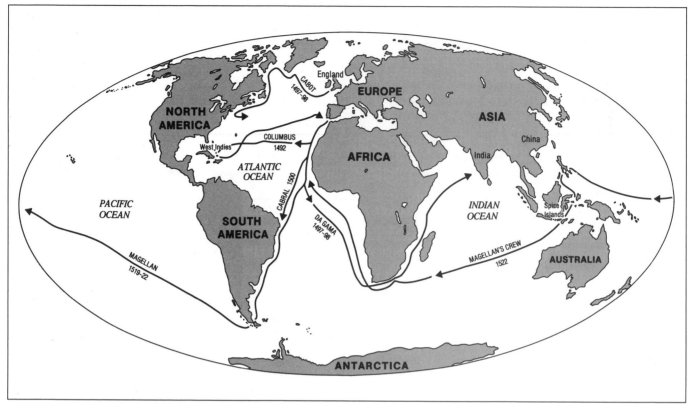

Early voyages of exploration

Christopher Columbus

Christopher Columbus set sail from Spain in August of 1492. He was not out to prove that the world was round, as stories often tell. He was not out to conquer new lands. Columbus was looking for a water route to India. He believed that by sailing west he might find a shorter route to the treasures of India. He had convinced Queen Isabella of Spain to support his voyage. So Queen Isabella and King Ferdinand gave Columbus three ships: the *Niña*, the *Pinta*, and the *Santa Maria*.

Columbus sailed westward. But instead of reaching India, Columbus landed on an island in the Bahamas. There it was; a new world where no land should have been! Columbus claimed the land in the name of Spain. And he named the land San Salvador.

Columbus thought he had reached an island off the coast of India. So he called the peaceful natives "Indians." It was not too many years before people realized Columbus was wrong about the land's location. But natives of the Americas are still called Indians. And those islands that Columbus discovered are called the "West Indies."

Many places in the Americas have been named after Columbus. But the word "America" comes from the name of another explorer, Amerigo Vespucci. Columbus had reached the West Indies. But Vespucci claimed to be the first European to reach the mainland of South America, in 1497.

Columbus arriving in the West Indies, October 12, 1492

Portuguese Explorers

Other explorers searched for that water route to India. The Spaniards and the Portuguese led the way in voyages of discovery.

In 1497 Vasco da Gama sailed around Africa's Cape of Good Hope. Vasco da Gama was a Portuguese nobleman and sailor. He became the first explorer to reach India by a sea route.

Another Portuguese explorer, Pedro Cabral, set out for India in 1500. He sailed wide of Africa and found Brazil. Thanks to Cabral, Brazil was claimed in the name of Portugal.

The Conquerors

Europeans quickly realized what a prize they had found in the new lands. No matter that people already lived there. No matter that the natives had civilizations and cultures of their own. Europeans thought the new lands were theirs for the taking.

When the Spanish **conquistadors** arrived in Mexico and South America, they found great civilizations. But the natives were no match for the greedy Europeans. The conquistadors brought guns and horses to help them claim gold.

Hernando Cortez, a Spaniard, attacked the Aztec capital of Tenochtitlan in 1521. The Spaniards soon conquered all of Mexico. They called it New Spain.

In South America, Francisco Pizarro attacked the Inca Empire in 1532. Again the natives were no match for the new enemy they did not understand. The Spaniards tried to make the Indians accept the Christian religion. Many Indians who refused were burned to death!

*Cortez conquering
the Aztecs*

The Spaniards treated the Indians cruelly in other ways, too. They used the Indians as slaves, working them harder than animals. After all, many Europeans thought, these people were only savages.

And the Europeans caused the Indians to suffer in yet another way. The Europeans brought their diseases with them to the Americas. Thousands of natives died from the new diseases.

The Slave Trade

In Africa, too, Europeans were treating people like work animals. The Europeans discovered that there was money to be made in slave trade. The Spanish and Portuguese brought ships full of Africans to the New World. The Africans were sold as slaves.

For a time the Spanish and Portuguese controlled the slave markets. Soon England and France joined the slave trade, too.

An Englishman, Sir John Hawkins, was one of the more famous slave traders. In the 1560s Hawkins made three voyages. On each he stopped in Africa to kidnap the strongest, healthiest men he could find. Then Hawkins carried the Africans to Spanish colonies in the New World. There he sold them as slaves. How could any decent person do such a thing, we might wonder. Yet Hawkins was known as a hero in England. Slave-trading led the way in setting up trade between England and the New World.

Around the World

Europeans set up new colonies and trading posts all around the world. There were European colonies in Asia, Africa, and the Americas.

In 1519 the Portuguese navigator Ferdinand Magellan began a voyage around the whole world. Magellan's own king had refused to back his trip. But the Spanish king agreed to supply five ships and 241 men.

Magellan sailed around South America and across the Pacific. However, Magellan himself did not make it all the way. In 1521 he was killed by natives in the Philippine Islands. Only one of the ships, the *Victoria*, completed the trip around the world. With only 18 survivors, it returned to Spain in 1522. This was the first ship to have sailed completely around the world. This voyage was the first proof that the Earth is round.

Pirates

When the English and French set sail for the New World, they were a little late. South American land had already been claimed. So they often resorted to **piracy** to claim their share of the treasures of South America.

Sir Frances Drake was an Englishman. He was the first Englishman to sail around the world. The English called him an explorer. The Spanish called him a pirate! Drake made daring attacks on Spanish ships in the West Indies. He invaded Spanish towns in the New World. He brought his treasures home to England.

The English loved him. But the Spaniards feared his piracy. They called him "The Dragon."

Settlers

The Spanish and Portuguese had already set up colonies in South America. So the English and French settled in North America. But this was hardly a blessing for the natives of North America.

The first Europeans landed on the east coast of North America. There they found hundreds of tribes of natives living peacefully. Each tribe had its own customs and culture. Most of the tribes lived in small villages. They lived by growing corn and other vegetables. But they didn't fit in with the newcomers. The Europeans brought new ways, new religions, and new diseases. The Indians became strangers in their own land.

In 1607 a group of English colonists settled in Jamestown in Virginia. Another group of English arrived on the sailing ship *Mayflower* in 1620. They landed at Plymouth, Massachusetts. They were pilgrims, and they were seeking religious freedom. Another religious group from England was the **Puritans**. They built several settlements on Massachusetts Bay in the 1630s.

More Europeans came. They were after religious freedom, a better life, and some adventure.

Most of the colonists were farmers. In the south, tobacco became a money-making crop. Slave traders brought black slaves from Africa to help on the tobacco plantations.

The first Thanksgiving dinner: Pilgrims and Indians

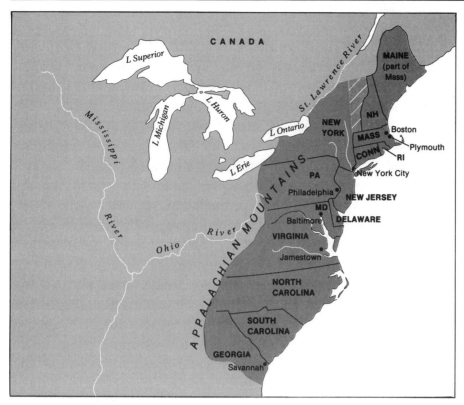

The thirteen original colonies

The settlers on North America's east coast formed 13 colonies. The colonies were under the control of the English government. Trade with Europe helped the colonies grow. Port towns like Boston sprang up.

The Indians and the Europeans did not live side by side. Slowly, the native Americans were driven westward. Over time they lost their lands to the newcomers.

Traders

Not all of the people who came to America were interested in settling and farming. There were also the **trappers**. These men made their living hunting animals and selling the furs. Many Frenchmen trapped along the Mississippi River. They explored the area, claiming lands in the name of France.

Many French trappers went north to Canada. Hunting was good there, and fishing too.

The English also held land in Canada. This land had been claimed by John Cabot in 1497. Sometimes fights over Canadian land broke out between the French and the English. In 1608 the French founded the Canadian settlement of Quebec. In 1759 the English captured that settlement. By 1763 the English had taken all of Canada from the French.

Trading Companies

Trade between Europe and the New World became big business. Merchants set up trading companies. The trading companies offered shares of their **stock** for sale. Sea voyages were expensive. So the **shareholders' investments** helped pay for the trips. Profits from successful trips were divided among the shareholders. In 1613 the Amsterdam Stock Exchange was built. This was the first building meant just for the buying and selling of stocks.

Three European countries became leaders in trade: Holland, England, and France. These were the trading powers of the 1600s. Banks were set up to help pay for trading trips. They lent money to the merchants and charged a fee called **interest**. London and Amsterdam became important banking cities.

Shipping could be a risky business. There were storms and shipwrecks and lost cargoes. While merchants could make a lot of money, they could also lose everything. **Insurance** companies backed up their businesses. The merchants paid the insurance companies a fee. Then if their ships were lost at sea or attacked by pirates, the insurance companies covered the losses.

Trade was heavy between Europe and the New World. There was also much trade between Europe and the East Indies. Three trading companies became powerful forces. These were the English East India Company, the Dutch East India Company, and the French East India Company. They brought home ships loaded with spices and rice, diamonds and ivory.

On a trading trip to the East Indies, Dutch sailors discovered the continent of Australia. They called their discovery New Holland. But the Dutch had little luck settling there.

The New Middle Class

European merchants became very wealthy. They often lived in the style of noblemen. They built grand houses in the cities or settled on country estates.

With their new-found wealth, many became vain and greedy. They were interested only in money and fashion and fine living. Other merchants used their own good fortune to help others. There were still plenty of poor people in the cities. So wealthy merchants paid to set up hospitals, orphanages, and schools.

Successful trade ventures created a new, rising middle class in Europe.

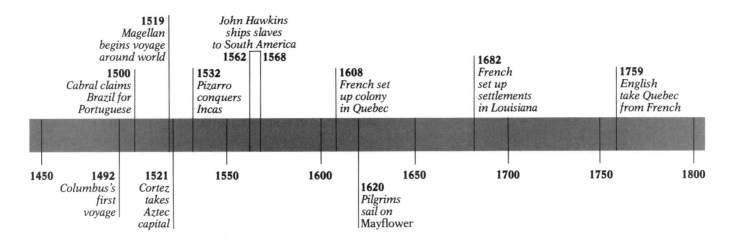

Points to Remember

◆ Columbus was looking for a sea route to India when he discovered the New World.

◆ The Spanish and Portuguese led the way in early explorations.

◆ Spanish conquistadors like Cortez and Pizarro claimed lands and gold for Spain.

◆ Africans were brought to the New World to be sold as slaves.

◆ While the Spanish and Portuguese set up colonies in South America, the English and French settled in North America.

◆ French trappers explored the Mississippi River and lands in Canada.

◆ England and France fought over lands in Canada.

◆ Holland, England, and France set up big trading companies.

◆ Successful trade created a new, wealthy middle class in Europe.

Think About It!

1. Why did Columbus call the natives of the New World "Indians"?

2. What happened to the Aztecs and the Incas?

3. How did the American colonists treat the Indians?

4. Why do you think that Europeans considered Africans and American Indians "savages"?

5. Why did trading companies buy "insurance"?

6. How did the great increase in trade change things in Europe?

Chapter 2

The Road to Revolution and Democracy

Words to Know

commonwealth   a nation in which the people hold the ruling power; a republic or democracy

council   a group of people that meet to decide something or to give advice

declaration   a public statement

divine   of or having to do with God or a god; like a god

independence   freedom from control by others

patriots   people who are loyal to their own country and show a great love for that country

petition   a written request, often with many signatures, to a person or group in authority

representation   sending one or more people to speak for the rights of others before a body of the government

Look for the answers as you read:

1. What ideas sprang from the Age of Reason?

2. How did the English Parliament system begin? How did it operate?

3. What led to civil war in England?

4. What was the Glorious Revolution? How did it gain more power for Parliament?

5. What complaints did colonists in America have against King George III and England?

6. What freedoms and rights did Americans win?

The Age of Reason

"**P**eople have certain natural rights! They are entitled to life, liberty, and property!"

"Man is born free! A monarch's right to rule is given to him not by God but by the people!"

"If a monarch rules badly, throw him out!"

Whoever heard of such wild ideas! These were shocking things to say in seventeenth-century Europe. And it took brave people to say them. Yet in the 1600s and 1700s, such ideas *were* being written and spoken in Europe. It was a time called the "Enlightenment" or the "Age of Reason."

Philosophers at that time believed that every person is born with the ability to reason. Everyone had the power to decide what was true or false, or good or bad. And they said that people should use their abilities to question things. Why were things the way they were? How might they be better? Why should one person have so much power over others?

Questions like those above were asked by the Englishman John Locke and the Frenchmen Voltaire and Jean Jacques Rousseau. These men were thinkers. They believed in freedom of thought, of action, and of speech. Their writings spread ideas of democracy and equality throughout the world. Their questions sparked flames of revolution in Europe and in America.

"Our lives could be better," people said. "Give us power over our own lives!"

John Locke

Voltaire

Jean Jacques Rousseau

The Road to Revolution in England

The Great Council of King Edward I, 1295

In 1215 King John of England was forced to sign the Magna Carta. This document limited certain powers of monarchs, and it granted certain rights. Mainly, it served to ensure the rights of nobles. It did little for the common people. Yet the ideas in the Magna Carta marked the beginning of democracy in England.

Now a king or queen could not simply go ahead and order new taxes. He or she first had to bring the matter before a **council** of nobles. That council was called the Great Council.

In 1272 King Edward I became King of England. In 1295, when Edward needed more money to fight a war, he called the Great Council into session. But Edward made some changes. He invited not only nobles to the Council, but also businessmen, knights, and rich landowners. Now more people had a voice in the king's decisions.

Parliament

The Great Council became known as Parliament. The word parliament comes from a French word, *parler*. It means "to speak." Members of Parliament could speak out, advise the king, and affect his decisions.

After 1295 Parliament was divided into two parts. One group, called the House of Lords, was made up of nobles. Members of the middle class were people such as merchants and rich farmers. They met in a group called the House of Commons. For those first few hundred years, the House of Lords held the most power. But the day would come when the House of Commons became the real law-making body.

King Charles I Does Away with Parliament

The power of Parliament grew and grew. Some kings didn't like it! King Charles I ruled England from 1625 until 1649. He did not want Parliament limiting his power.

In 1603 the line of Stuart kings had begun with the reign of James I. King Charles I was the son of James. He believed in the "**divine** right" of kings. He believed that God gave him the right to rule. He also thought he should rule with absolute power.

Parliament buildings on the Thames River, London

King Charles decided to ask people to pay higher taxes. When people did not pay the high taxes he demanded, he had them thrown in jail.

Parliament did not like it. "What about the Magna Carta?" they asked. "Rulers must have our approval on new taxes!"

In 1628 Parliament presented King Charles with a **Petition** of Right. The petition said that a king could not demand new taxes without Parliament's consent. It also said the king could not throw people in jail without a jury trial.

King Charles agreed to the petition. But Charles did not keep his word. He kept raising taxes. When Parliament protested, Charles I disbanded the whole group! King Charles ruled without a parliament from 1629 until 1640.

Then trouble developed with Scotland. Charles I had been forcing the Scottish to follow the English religion. Scotland rebelled. So Charles called Parliament back into session in 1640. He wanted Parliament to provide money to go to war with Scotland.

Again Parliament tried to put reins on the king's power. Charles I reacted by arresting five of the leading members of Parliament. The king's troops marched right into a session of Parliament and made the arrest!

It was too much. The people rebelled.

Civil War in England

In 1642 a civil war began in England. It lasted until 1649. The nobles who supported the king were called "Royalists." The greatest supporters of Parliament were the Puritans. They were called "Roundheads" because they cut their hair short.

A man named Oliver Cromwell became a leading figure in the civil war. Cromwell was a member of Parliament. He led the Puritan army against the king.

Cromwell's military victories meant the end of King Charles's reign. In 1649 Charles I was captured and tried by Parliament. He was found to be a "public enemy of the nation." Charles I was beheaded.

Cromwell at the Battle of Marston Moor

The Commonwealth and Oliver Cromwell

Parliament set up a republic. The republic, known as the **Commonwealth** of England, lasted from 1649 until 1660. Under the Commonwealth, England had no monarch. The country was governed by a committee of Parliament and its leader, Oliver Cromwell.

But Cromwell fought with Parliament. To solve the arguments, he put an end to Parliament in 1653. For the rest of the commonwealth period, Cromwell ruled England alone.

Cromwell had believed in freedom. He had refused the title of king when Parliament once offered it to him. He had been against the total power of kings. Now he had sole power in England. Cromwell's

Cromwell dissolving Parliament

official title was Lord Protector of the Commonwealth. During his rule, he brought Ireland and Scotland under English control.

Oliver Cromwell died in 1658. His son Richard tried to carry on his father's policies. But Richard was not as strong as his father. And the people of England were ready to return to the royal Stuart line.

The Glorious Revolution

In 1660 Charles II became king. He restored Parliament, and things were quiet for a while. But new problems came up when James II came to the throne after Charles III.

Parliament was unhappy with King James II. He asked for too much power. So Parliament sent word to James II's daughter Mary and her husband William of Orange. Parliament asked them to come from Holland and take over James II's throne.

Did this anger King James? Did it cause another war? No. James II left the throne quietly. It was a bloodless takeover. Parliament persuaded William and Mary to sign over many of their royal rights and powers. The change came to be called the "Glorious Revolution."

In 1689 William and Mary signed a Bill of Rights. With that, England took another big step toward true democracy. Now Parliament was truly the main force in government.

One day the Americans would write their own Bill of Rights. The English Bill of Rights would serve as their model.

Parliament offering the crown to William and Mary

Changes in Parliament

Over time, Parliament itself became more democratic. By the late 1600s, the House of Lords held less power. The House of Commons held more. Members of the House of Lords still inherited their positions. But House of Commons members were elected by the people.

Revolution in America

George III became king of England in 1760. When he came to the throne, England had colonies in North America. George asked for the loyalty of his subjects in the New World. They seemed happy to give that loyalty.

But George III had wars to pay for, too. In 1763 the French and Indian War ended in America. The Americans and British had defeated the French and some Indian tribes. That war had cost a lot of money. Someone had to pay the bills. So King George demanded high taxes from his subjects in the colonies.

"High taxes, but no rights!" the American colonists complained. They had seen that people had won new rights in England. They read the words of Locke, Rousseau, and Voltaire. The Americans wanted rights and freedom, too.

"No taxation without **representation**!" was their cry. If they paid taxes to King George, they wanted a say in his government.

And some Americans wanted more than representation. There were men like Samuel Adams; men who didn't want representation at all. They wanted freedom!

Americans were willing to fight for that freedom. **Patriots** like Thomas Jefferson spoke out for liberty. Jefferson used his pen to fight for **independence**. He wrote that Parliament had no right to control the colonies. And he said that unfair acts by the king meant the colonists owed him no loyalty!

The signing of the Declaration of Independence, July 4, 1776

The colonies asked Jefferson to write a **declaration** of independence.

"All men are created equal," the declaration said. "A government must govern fairly or the people have a right to change it."

On July 4, 1776, the Declaration of Independence was approved. King George sent troops to the colonies. The colonists had to fight the English for their independence. General George Washington led the fight. Washington would later become the first president of the new United States of America.

Other lands watched as Americans won their freedom. They witnessed the birth of a new nation. That nation promised its people freedom of speech, of religion, and of the press. It promised a voice in government. It promised trial by jury. And it spoke of equality.

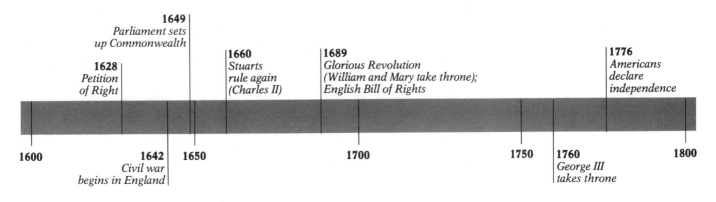

Points to Remember

◆ Ideas of freedom, equality, and fairness of rule came out of the Age of Reason.

◆ English Parliament helped limit the powers of the monarch.

◆ There are two houses of Parliament: the House of Lords and the House of Commons.

◆ Some rulers did not like asking Parliament to allow them to raise taxes.

◆ During England's civil war, Oliver Cromwell supported Parliament in overthrowing the king.

◆ After the war, Cromwell headed the English Commonwealth for nine years.

◆ With the return to Stuart kings came the Glorious Revolution. It was a bloodless takeover of the throne by Mary, of the Stuart line, and her husband, William of Orange.

◆ The Glorious Revolution brought still more power for Parliament and a Bill of Rights for the English people.

◆ English colonists in America had thoughts of freedom, too, and they were angered by King George's high taxes.

◆ In 1776 the American colonists declared their independence. They fought a war and won their freedom.

Think About It!

1. How did Voltaire, Locke, and Rousseau influence England and America?

2. How were the new ideas of the Age of Reason the opposite of the idea of the divine right of kings?

3. What kind of problems did Parliament have with Stuart kings?

4. How did the Glorious Revolution put England on the road to democracy?

5. How was Parliament different from the earlier Great Council?

6. What led to revolution in America? Who were some of the leaders of the American Revolution?

Chapter 3

Revolution in France

Words to Know

arsenal   a place where guns and ammunition are stored

betraying   giving help to the enemy; being unfaithful to; for example, *betraying* one's own country

colonial   having settlements in far-off lands; for example, Great Britain was a *colonial* power because it ruled colonies in many parts of the world

dictator   a ruler who has total power

dungeons   dark, underground rooms used as prisons

fortress   a building with strong walls for defense against an enemy

fraternity   brotherhood

guillotine   an instrument used for cutting off a person's head; it has two posts crossed by a heavy blade

motto   a word or phrase that expresses goals, ideas, or ideals

oath   a serious promise, often pledged in the name of God

riot   a violent disturbance created by a crowd of people

symbol   an object that stands for an idea; for example, the dove is a *symbol* of peace

turmoil   a condition of great confusion

Look for the answers as you read:

1. How did the Age of Reason and the American Revolution lead to revolution in France?

2. What were the Three Estates?

3. Where did the French National Assembly hold its first meeting, and what did the Assembly decide?

4. How did the storming of the Bastille lead to a bloody, lawless rebellion?

5. How did the rest of Europe react to the French Revolution?

6. How did Napoleon Bonaparte gain leadership in France, and how was he defeated?

France, in the early 1700s, had a government that was still locked into the Middle Ages. French kings ruled by "divine right." They considered their thrones a right given to them by God. No matter how unfair the rule, French people had to accept it. King Louis XIV is said to have declared, "I am the State."

Nobles led lives of luxury. They lived in fine palaces paid for by taxes collected from the lower and middle classes. While the nobles lived splendidly, the peasants often went without enough to eat.

The Age of Reason in France

The coronation of King Louis XVI

But by the 1780s, Frenchmen were listening to new ideas. They read the works of Rousseau and Voltaire. "Look at England," the writers said. "The people there are free. Look at America, at their successful fight for freedom. We, too, deserve some rights!" Political conditions did not yet show it. But the Age of Reason had come to France.

The French had helped the Americans in their war for independence from British rule. French nobles were happy to see the British defeated by anyone. French peasants liked the idea of a fight against tyranny. The Frenchman, Lafayette, went to America and joined the colonists' battle. George Washington gave Lafayette command of a division, and the two fought side by side.

When the Americans won their war, the French began thinking about freedom for themselves.

The Estates-General

King Louis XVI

By 1788 trouble was brewing in France. The peasants and the middle class were unhappy. The government was in trouble, too. The king was out of money. Fancy living and too many wars had resulted in an empty treasury.

In 1789 King Louis XVI called a meeting of the Estates-General. This was a government body something like Parliament. The Estates-General had not met for 175 years. Now there was to be a meeting at Versailles. This was the name of King Louis's fine palace just outside of Paris. King Louis wanted the Estates-General to grant him more money in new taxes.

Three groups of people made up the Estates-General. Each group was called an "estate." The First Estate included wealthy clergymen. They arrived at King Louis's meeting dressed in fine clothing and riding in beautiful carriages.

Members of the Second Estate were the nobles. Many were wealthy and came from large country manors. Some of the noblemen, however, had lost most of their wealth. They had only their titles left.

The First and Second Estates represented only a tiny part of the French population. Most of the people were represented by the Third Estate. The Third Estate included a middle class made up of merchants and city workers. And the Third Estate included the peasants of France.

Each of the three estates had *one* vote in meetings. This was hardly fair since the Third Estate represented 98 percent of the population. The First and Second Estates could band together. And they could outvote the Third Estate every time they wanted to. Members of the Third Estate were ready for change.

At the 1789 meeting in Versailles, the Third Estate asked for more votes. King Louis XVI refused.

Marie Antoinette

The Third Estate rebelled. The members called their own meeting. They declared themselves the National Assembly of France. The king refused to give them a government meeting hall. So the Third Estate held its own meeting at a nearby tennis court.

At the meeting, members of the Third Estate took the Tennis Court **Oath**. They swore that they would give France a constitution. At this point, Louis XVI gave in. He said that he would accept the National Assembly. He said that he would divide votes more fairly among the three estates.

In the meantime, the king was organizing his troops. When he gathered an army near an assembly meeting, people began to worry. Was the king planning to stop the National Assembly by force? The people grew angry. Force, they said, would be met by force! France was now approaching the boiling point.

The Tennis Court Meeting

To the people of Paris, the Bastille was a terrible **symbol**. It stood for the tyranny of their king and for the injustices they faced. The Bastille was a gloomy **fortress** built in 1370. It was used as a prison. All that was needed to throw a Frenchman into prison was the say-so of the king.

The Bastille was a dark, mysterious place. People were locked away there for disagreeing with the king or for failing to pay taxes. There were stories of men rotting away in the Bastille's dark **dungeons** and of terrible tortures. Actually, under earlier kings the prison had done away with dungeons and tortures. But the horror stories remained. Most Frenchmen hated and feared the Bastille.

On July 14, 1789, a **riot** broke out in Paris. The people had become alarmed by the king's gathering troops. They decided it was time to make a stand for freedom. They would attack that symbol of the king's unjust powers—the hated Bastille.

Early in the day, a mob of rioters broke into an **arsenal**. They took muskets and cannons. Then they attacked. "Down with the Bastille!" the excited rebels shouted. There was no stopping the mob. They murdered the governor of the prison. They carried his head on a stick through the streets.

The rebels then took the keys to the prison as their prize. They unlocked the doors to find only seven prisoners inside! But the Bastille had fallen, and the Revolution had begun.

The Storming of the Bastille

The storming of the Bastille, July 14, 1789

On this same day, the king returned to his palace at Versailles after a day of hunting. Communication was slow in the eighteenth century. So he knew nothing of the riots and murders. It had been poor hunting that day. No deer had been killed. And so King Louis wrote only one word in his diary on July 14, 1789. He wrote *Rien*, a French word meaning "nothing."

The day that King Louis wrote "nothing" was a day that France would always remember!

The French Revolution

Revolutionaries throughout France were excited by the storming of the Bastille. They began their own riots for freedom. In October a group of women set out from Paris. They tried to attack the royal family in the palace at Versailles. The king's guard had to keep order.

Peasants rose up against federal lords. Many noblemen did not feel safe in France. They fled the country.

During the next two years, 1789–1791, the National Assembly wrote the new constitution it had promised. New laws were made doing away with the feudal system. The nobles lost most of their rights and privileges. The king lost much of his power. And the old system of taxes was ended.

On August 26, 1789, the National Assembly wrote the Declaration of the Rights of Man. It was based on the English Bill of Rights and the American Declaration of Independence.

"Liberty, Equality, and Fraternity!"

Rulers throughout Europe saw what was happening in France. They were frightened. They worried that ideas of revolution could spread to their lands. So rulers of Austria and Prussia sent armies into France to try to crush the Revolution.

The leaders of the French Revolution were outraged. They thought that their own king had called for the outside armies. They accused Louis XVI of **betraying** France. They forced him out of office. And they held elections for a new lawmaking body called the "National Convention."

In 1792 the National Convention declared France a republic. The **motto** of the new republic was "Liberty, Equality, and **Fraternity**!"

The Reign of Terror

Leaders of the new republic became fearful of their enemies. Their main goal was to seek out those enemies and do away with them. The revolution became bloodier.

Revolutionaries found King Louis XVI guilty of betraying his country. In 1793 Louis XVI and his queen, Marie Antoinette, were executed. Throughout 1793 and 1794, the new leaders of France arrested and executed many people. Anyone suspected of being against the Republic was attacked. It was a time known as the Reign of Terror. "Off with their heads!" became the cry of that stage of the French Revolution.

A Frenchman had invented the **guillotine**, a machine for quickly cutting off heads! Hundreds of suspected enemies of the revolution were beheaded. Carts rolled through the streets of Paris, carrying victims to the guillotine.

The guillotine:
Execution of Robespierre

A man named Robespierre was one of the most violent leaders of the Revolution. Robespierre believed the Republic would never be safe as long as one enemy lived. Later, the people turned on Robespierre himself. After sentencing so many others to death, Robespierre lost his own head to the French guillotine.

The country was in a **turmoil**. The leaders of the Revolution could not control the people or organize the government. The fighting and bloodshed went on and on.

The Revolution had created a strong, new army. That army drove Austrian and Prussian forces out of France. One of the officers in the French army was a young man named Napoleon Bonaparte.

Meanwhile, the National Convention of France had been growing steadily weaker. In October 1795 it came under attack by an army of 30,000 national guardsmen. The guardsmen wanted to get rid of the National Convention and bring back the monarchy. The Convention called on General Napoleon Bonaparte to put down the uprising. Napoleon, a general at age 26, proved his military worth. On October 5, 1795, he brought in a battery of cannons. The uprising was ended "with a whiff of grapeshot," he said.

The Directory soon replaced the National Convention in the leadership of France. As Napoleon won battles and gained power, the Directory began to worry. Was Napoleon trying to become the sole ruler of all of France?

That is exactly what Napoleon did. He pushed out the Directory. And in 1799 he made himself **dictator** of France. One of the first things Napoleon did as ruler was to set up the Napoleonic Code. This was a new constitution which contained a single set of laws for all of France and its territories. The Napoleonic Code remains to this day as the basis of French law.

France soon discovered that Napoleon was a good politician as well as a good soldier. Napoleon put himself directly in charge of the army. He brought a quick end to the fighting within France. He set up a police force responsible only to him. He invited back the nobles who had fled France during the Revolution. "You will be safe," Napoleon told them, "if you are loyal to me."

Napoleon Bonaparte

Napoleon Bonaparte

France Under Napoleon

Napoleon put an end to the French Republic that the revolution had won. In 1804 Napoleon had himself crowned emperor. He then crowned his wife, Josephine, empress. He let his ambition and desire for power spread war across Europe. But he did make some good changes in the French government. Napoleon changed unfair tax laws. He required all people, rich and poor, to pay taxes under the same laws. The rich received no favors. Napoleon also strengthened and reorganized the French schools.

But everything, including education, religion, and the press, was subject to strict government control. And the French government *was* Napoleon!

Napoleon had a strong, wealthy France behind him now. He had the loyalty of the people. He now set out to conquer a European empire. He led France into war with Great Britain and most of the rest of Europe. Napoleon was a clever general. He won battle after battle. By 1812 Napoleon controlled most of Europe. Only Britain could not be conquered by Napoleon's armies.

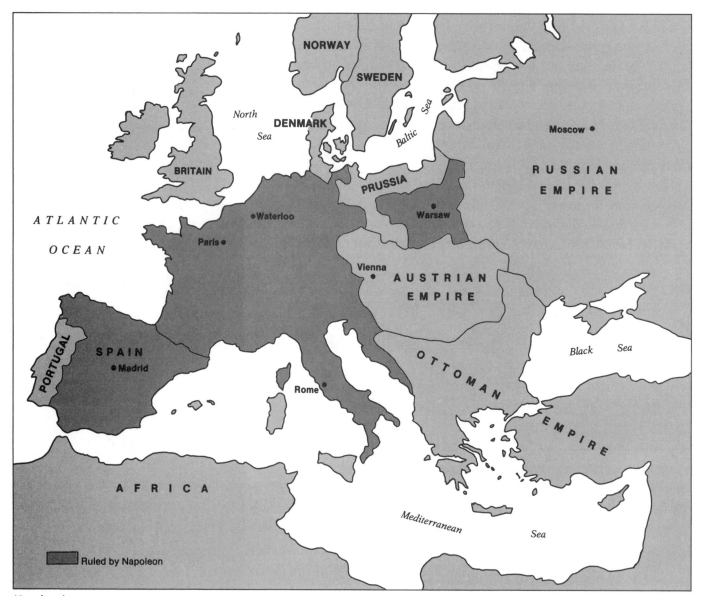

Napoleon's empire

Napoleon's Mistake

In 1812, Napoleon declared war on Russia. He attacked with an army of nearly 600,000 men. He won a major victory over the Russians at the battle of Borodino. But the Russian armies were clever. They fled eastward, leading Napoleon's men on a chase deep into the heart of Russia. As the Russians retreated, they destroyed everything of value in Napoleon's path.

When Napoleon and his army reached Moscow, they found a deserted city. Most of the people had fled. Those who stayed behind set fire to the city. The French soon found themselves occupying a city of ruins.

Then winter came. It was an icy Russian winter. Napoleon's army had almost run out of food. They were starving. They were freezing. There was only one thing to do. Napoleon gave the orders to head for home. The Russians attacked again and again as Napoleon's weakened forces struggled toward France. The French suffered terrible losses during the retreat from Russia. Over 500,000 men

Napoleon's retreat from Moscow

either were killed, or died of illness or starvation. Others deserted or were captured. Many simply froze to death. The attack on Russia was Napoleon's mistake.

The End for Napoleon

Other countries took heart when they heard of France's defeat in Russia. Napoleon could be beaten! These countries joined together. Prussia, Sweden, and Spain joined with Great Britain and Russia to march against Napoleon.

The French saw that their emperor was beaten. So the French Senate turned against him. They called for a new king to rule France. On April 11, 1814, Napoleon gave up his throne. Louis XVIII was crowned King of France. Napoleon was exiled. The king sent him to the little island of Elba off the coast of Italy.

Napoleon was not a man who gave up easily. In less than a year, he escaped from Elba and returned to France. There he found supporters and actually ruled France again for 100 days. But Napoleon could not hold on to his power. This time the English outnumbered and defeated Napoleon at the battle of Waterloo on June 18, 1815. The English army was under the command of the Duke of Wellington.

Again Napoleon was sent away as a prisoner. The English sent him to far-off Saint Helena. This was a tiny island off the west coast of Africa. It was there on May 5, 1821, that Napoleon died.

France After Napoleon

A royal line of kings ruled in France once more. And then again, there was revolution. For the next 55 years, France saw change after change; three revolutions in all. There was a Second Republic, a Second Empire, and then, in 1870, a Third Republic.

Under the Third Republic, France built a **colonial** empire. French colonies around the world strengthened trade and industry. France's Third Republic lasted until World War II, when Germany took over France.

After World War II a Fourth Republic was set up and then a Fifth. Social revolution continued. Women struggled to take their place in society, to hold property, and to take jobs. Minority groups looked for work, for fair pay, and for good housing. The French still worked toward "Liberty, Equality, and Fraternity."

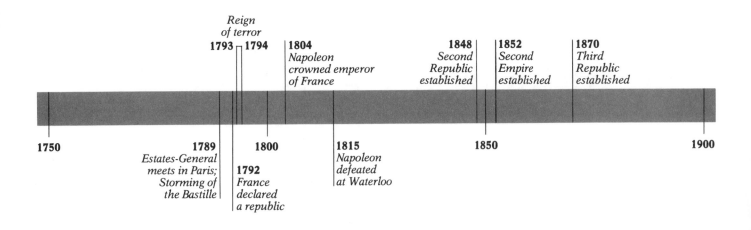

Points to Remember

◆ The Age of Reason and the American War of Independence gave Frenchmen ideas of fighting for their own freedom.

◆ French kings, like Louis XVI, believed that they ruled by "divine right."

◆ The Third Estate of the French Estates-General represented all the common people.

◆ A National Assembly met in 1789 and decided that France should have a constitution.

◆ The French Revolution officially began on July 14, 1789, with the storming of the Bastille.

◆ A Reign of Terror from 1793–1794 led to turmoil and bloodshed.

◆ Napoleon Bonaparte stepped in to restore order in France.

◆ Napoleon's ambition led him to become emperor of France and to conquer much of Europe.

◆ Napoleon met final defeat at Waterloo in 1815.

◆ The French government underwent several other changes in a series of social and political revolutions.

Think About It!

1. How was France affected by the American Revolution?

2. What groups made up each of the Three Estates that met in Versailles in 1789?

3. Why did the Third Estate feel it was getting cheated?

4. How do the Three Estates compare with the British Parliament and its two houses?

5. What three words made up the motto of the French Revolution? What do they mean?

6. What countries tried to crush the French Revolution? Why did they fear revolution?

7. What were some of the useful things that Napoleon Bonaparte did for France?

Chapter 4

The Industrial Revolution

Words to Know

factories   buildings where goods are made by machinery

imperialism   the practice of conquering other lands, forming colonies in other lands, or controlling the government and wealth of weaker lands

imported   brought into one country from another

industry   business and manufacturing

investors   those who expect to make a profit by lending money to a business

labor unions   groups of workers joined together to protect their wages, working conditions, and job benefits

looms   machines for weaving thread or yarn into cloth

natural resources   materials that are provided by nature, such as forests, minerals, and water

raw materials   matter in its natural condition, not changed by some human process

shuttle   a device in weaving that carries thread back and forth between threads that go up and down

textile   cloth or fabric made by weaving

transportation   the act of carrying from one place to another

Look for the answers as you read:

1. What is an industrial revolution?

2. Why did the Industrial Revolution begin in Great Britain?

3. How did the English textile industry change?

4. How did the Industrial Revolution encourage imperialism?

5. How did the Industrial Revolution improve people's lives?

6. How did it lower the quality of life?

7. How did the Industrial Revolution make countries more dependent on each other?

The name "Industrial Revolution" is used to describe one of the biggest changes in history. It describes the time when people went from making goods by hand to making them with machines.

Before the 1700s most goods were made by hand. Individual workers crafted tools and jewelry, cloth and housewares. Any machines that were used were small, simple, and privately owned. Work was done in homes or in small workshops.

Before 1750 any changes in production methods came slowly. But after 1750, those changes were rapid. The changes in the ways goods were produced happened fast enough to be called a "revolution."

The most dramatic changes in industry began in Great Britain in about 1750. Scientists, it is true, had been inventing things during earlier years. But most of their work centered around theories and ideas. Now science and invention took a more practical turn. Inventors developed machines especially designed to increase production of goods and to help people make a profit.

The Industrial Revolution began in Great Britain for a number of reasons. For one thing, Britain had a large supply of workers. Women, as well as men, were ready to leave their homes and join the industrial force.

Great Britain Leads the Industrial Revolution

Women working in a pen factory

Great Britain also had the **natural resources** needed for **industry**. Britain had a good supply of coal and iron. Coal could produce the energy to keep the new steam engines running. And coal was needed to produce iron. Iron could be used to improve machines and tools. And it could be used to build railroad tracks, bridges, and ships.

Britain had the **transportation** that industry needed. Products had to be marketed and moved. Steam locomotives and ocean-going steamships were developed in Britain.

Britain had **investors**. These were people with money to back the new businesses.

Britain had colonies to serve as ready markets for the goods. British colonies also supplied **raw materials**, like cotton, to the **factories** in London and other cities. And the British government was eager to support growing industry.

For all these reasons, Great Britain saw a burst of industrial development. In the late 1700s and 1800s, Britain became known as the "Workshop of the World."

The Textile Industry

Britain's **textile** industry produced cloth. This industry is a good example of what the early Industrial Revolution was all about.

In the earliest days, British merchants **imported** cloth from other lands. Because of the costs of shipping finished goods, cloth was very expensive.

Later, in the 1600s, Britain began importing raw cotton. The British spun their own threads and then wove their own cloth.

Farm families did the work. They set up spinning wheels and **looms** in their cottages. Both spinning wheel and loom were operated by hand. The families who worked this way were called "cottage weavers."

Merchants would buy the finished cloth from the cottage weavers. The amounts of cloth produced were never very large. In order to meet their own needs, the weavers had to farm land, too. They could only make cloth in their spare time. There was never enough finished cloth for all the people who wanted to buy it. So English businessmen looked for ways to improve and increase the production of textiles.

Woman spinning

In the 1700s some new machines were invented that changed the textile industry. Spinners and weavers left their cottages and went to work in new factories.

The first important invention in the textile-making revolution was the "flying **shuttle**." In 1733 a man named John Kay invented a shuttle; a device on a loom. The shuttle made it possible to weave wider pieces of cloth. Now one worker could do the work of two.

Soon more cotton yarn was needed than could be produced. Businessmen offered prizes to the inventor of a machine to spin yarn. In 1764 James Hargreaves came up with just such a machine. He named it after his wife. The "spinning jenny" used the same idea as the spinning wheel. But it could spin as many as 80 threads at one time.

New Inventions Move Textile Making Out of the Cottages

Woman using a spinning jenny

Young girl spinning at a frame

The biggest change came in 1769. Then Richard Arkwright invented a machine called the "water frame." Now even more cotton thread could be spun at once. The water frame ran by water power. It was big; so big that it could not fit into a cottage. It was also an expensive piece of machinery. The water frame required a special building of its own.

And so the textile business moved out of the English cottages. Mills and factories were built. Workers were no longer their own bosses. They became factory hands. They worked in large mills that often employed up to 600 people.

In 1779 Samuel Crompton combined the spinning jenny and the water frame into one machine. He called it the "mule." The mule could spin much finer threads very rapidly.

Now the weavers had to keep step with the spinners. With so much thread being produced, the textile industry needed a better loom. In 1785 Edmund Cartwright invented a steam-powered loom.

Workers sometimes feared the new machines. Would the machines completely replace the workers? Would they lose their jobs? At one point, antimachine riots broke out. Mobs smashed machines, shouting, "Men, not machines!" Sometimes progress was a frightening thing. But the revolution could not be stopped.

Within 50 years' time the textile industry had entirely changed. What had been a cottage industry had turned into a big business. And a way of life had changed, too, for thousands of textile workers.

The Steam Engine

New machines needed power. Water power was not strong enough to run heavy machines. During the 1600s inventors had begun experimenting with "fire engines," or steam engines. In 1698 Thomas Savery built the first commercial steam engine. Around 1712 Thomas Newcomen improved on Savery's engine. It was, however, far from perfect. It used too much coal.

In 1769 a Scottish engineer named James Watt invented an improved steam engine. For several years only the textile industry made use of Watt's engine. By 1850, however, it was being used throughout Britain. Then it spread throughout the rest of Europe.

Steam for Transportation

The invention of the steam engine completely changed transportation. In 1804 a British engineer, Richard Trevithick, built the first steam locomotive. Steam locomotives came into general use in Britain in the late 1830s. And by 1850, Great Britain had 6,600 miles of railroad track. The United States, France, and Germany built their own rail systems during the next ten years.

It was an American, Robert Fulton, who, in 1807, built the first successful steamboat. Within a few years, steamboats were being used on British rivers. And by the mid-1800s, steam-powered ships were carrying raw materials and finished goods across the ocean.

Early steam locomotive

The Industrial Revolution Changes Life: Imperialism

The Industrial Revolution meant new inventions and new products. It also meant new needs. As the ability to produce goods increased, so did the need for more raw materials. Britain needed even more coal to fire the steam engines. It needed more cotton to spin into thread. And it needed more iron to make railroad tracks and machinery.

Imperialism seemed to be a solution to the problems of getting raw materials. Britain took over territories in Africa and Asia and formed colonies there. The colonies could help supply Britain with the raw materials it needed. The colonies could also serve as a market for English goods. People living in the colonies bought finished products from Britain.

The Industrial Revolution Changes Life: The Workers

Did the Industrial Revolution improve the lives of the English people? Or did it make life harder? A look at life in England in the late 1700s and early 1800s gives a mixed picture.

In many ways life was better. Average incomes tripled between 1700 and 1815. Between 1815 and 1836, incomes increased 30 times over! People had better food to eat. They had more meat, more sugar and tea and coffee. Coal not only fueled the industrial machines, it also heated homes and cooked food.

Match-makers at a London factory

For the merchants, bankers, shipowners, and factory owners, the Industrial Revolution meant wealth. The middle class grew and took new power in British government.

New inventions in communication let people learn what was going on in their world. In 1837 Samuel F. B. Morse invented the telegraph. He also invented a code to send telegrams—the Morse code. By 1866 a telegraph cable reached across the Atlantic. Many such changes were amazing and wonderful.

But life did not improve for everyone. As the Industrial Revolution went on, life got harder for many city workers. People spent long days in dirty, dangerous factories, working for poor wages.

At first factory work paid well. But soon the owners found they could hire women and children for less wages than men. Soon most of the factory workers were women and children; often very young children. Wages dropped.

Many of the children working in factories came from orphanages or very poor families. They were treated much like slaves. They often had to work from five in the morning until eight at night. Some factory owners treated the children quite well. Others beat the young workers for such crimes as falling asleep at their work or working too slowly.

In the 1800s there were new laws called Factory Acts. These laws took the very youngest children out of the factories. The laws also put limits on the number of hours young people and women could work.

But there was no such thing then as safety measures or protection against industrial accidents. It is easy to imagine what happened to many little children working on dangerous machines with no safety devices.

Young boys working in a cotton mill

The Industrial Revolution Changes Life: The Cities

Britain's cities were becoming dark with ash from the new coal-burning factories. But these factories drew people to the cities. As a result, Great Britain's cities went through a population explosion. In 1801 about 78 percent of the people in Britain lived on farms. By 1901 about 75 percent lived in cities.

Where were all these people going to make their homes? Housing had to be built quickly and cheaply. The results were poorly built slum buildings. Inside were small apartments where whole families often shared one room. Sewage and garbage could not be disposed of properly. These conditions led to the outbreak and spread of disease.

It would not be long before people began to protest against this kind of life. They protested against factories that employed young children and paid terrible wages. And they protested against having to work with dangerous machines that had no safety devices.

The Industrial Revolution taught workers that they had to band together. They formed **labor unions** to demand better, fairer conditions. Of course factory owners were not in favor of the workers' unions. Until 1825 unions in Great Britain were against the law.

London slums, 1870s

Dudley Street, London, 1870s

The Industrial Revolution Spreads

Industrialization began in Great Britain. But during the 1800s, it spread to other parts of the world. France, Germany, the United States, and then Russia all began to industrialize. Then came Japan.

Japan became an industrial nation in a very short period of time. Between the late 1800s and 1914, Japan entered the modern world. It went from a medieval society, where all work was done by hand, to a highly industrialized nation. The government supported Japan's push toward industry, and the country saw rapid change.

Electricity

In 1831 an Englishman named Michael Faraday invented a machine called the "dynamo." It generated an electric current by using magnets. Faraday's discovery led to the building of more powerful electric generators and electric motors. In time the use of electricity as a source of power would become widespread.

Petroleum

In the 1850s Americans discovered that petroleum, or unrefined oil, could be used for many things. It could be used to make kerosene, and kerosene could be used for heat and light. Oil could make machinery run more smoothly. Fortunately, there was a good supply of crude oil available in the United States.

Oil was to become one of the most valuable resources in the world. This would come about with the invention of the internal combustion engine and the diesel engine. Petroleum could be turned into gasoline and diesel fuel to run those engines. The availability of oil would give nations new wealth and power.

Industrialization Makes Nations Work Together

Industrialization has forced nations of the world to depend on each other. Countries have had to work out trade agreements. The more industrialized countries often depend on other nations for raw materials. Less developed countries need finished products.

The United States, Germany, Japan, and England depend on Saudi Arabia, Mexico, Indonesia, and Nigeria for crude oil. They get uranium from nations in Africa. Chile and Peru, in South America, export copper.

The Industrial Revolution still makes itself felt all around the world. Some nations build the factories and produce the goods. Other nations profit from their plentiful natural resources.

The results of the revolution are all around us. They can be seen in British coal mines, in Japanese electronics factories, in cities, and on farms. The Industrial Revolution has changed the way people live and where they live. It has changed the way they depend on each other.

At one time, some people thought that the Industrial Revolution would come to an end. They thought that all the great changes and developments had already happened. In the late 1800s, it was actually suggested that the United States Patent Office be closed. Surely, some people thought, everything possible had already been invented. We know now that the revolution is far from over. New developments continue every day.

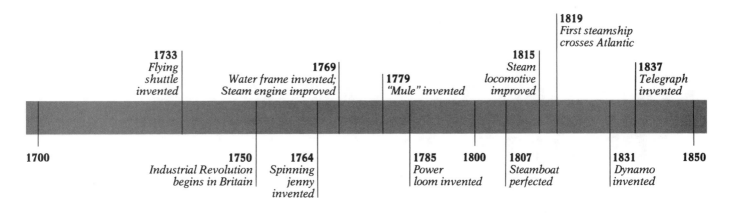

1733
Flying shuttle invented

1769
Water frame invented; Steam engine improved

1779
"Mule" invented

1815
Steam locomotive improved

1819
First steamship crosses Atlantic

1837
Telegraph invented

1700

1750
Industrial Revolution begins in Britain

1764
Spinning jenny invented

1785
Power loom invented

1800

1807
Steamboat perfected

1831
Dynamo invented

1850

Points to Remember

♦ During the Industrial Revolution, people went from making goods by hand to making goods by machine.

♦ Great Britain led the Industrial Revolution with rapid changes beginning around 1750.

♦ Britain's textile industry moved out of country cottages and into city factories.

♦ The invention of steam power revolutionized manufacturing and transportation.

♦ The need for raw materials caused Europeans to seek new colonies.

♦ Industrialization caused a rapid growth in city populations.

♦ Life for many improved. A strong, wealthy middle class grew.

♦ Life for many became harder. Working conditions were often unsafe and unhealthy, with men, women, and children working long hours.

♦ More and more countries industrialized over the years. Nations became dependent on each other for raw materials and finished products.

Think About It!

1. Why was Great Britain called the "Workshop of the World?"

2. Describe a typical English textile factory in the early 1800s. Describe the equipment and the workers one might find there.

3. Describe life in many English cities during the Industrial Revolution.

4. How did the Industrial Revolution lead to the growth of the middle class?

5. How did the Industrial Revolution affect English colonization in America, Africa, and Asia?

Chapter 5

The Changing World: Latin America

Words to Know

burros   small donkeys, usually used as pack animals

descendants   people who come from certain ancestors

discrimination   treating a person or people unfairly because of their race or religion

dominate   to be most important, most powerful, strongest

haciendas   large Spanish-style ranches or country homes

influence   the power to affect other people or things

liberator   one who frees a group of people

mural   a large picture painted on a wall

viceroy   the governor of a country or province, who rules as the representative of his king

Look for the answers as you read:

1. How did this area come to be called "Latin America"?

2. Who were the Creoles? Why were they ready to fight for independence?

3. Who were the mestizos? Why were they ready to fight for independence?

4. Who were some of the men who fought for independence in Latin America?

5. What kind of government existed in many of the new independent Latin American nations?

6. Latin American culture comes from a blend of which peoples?

Colonization

For 300 years Spaniards built colonies in the New World. From about 1500 until about 1800, they settled in Mexico, Central America, and South America. Some Portuguese settled in the eastern part of South America. And the French also founded a few settlements. But most of the lands fell to the Spanish. All the lands in this area are called "Latin America." That is because the Spanish, Portuguese, and French languages came from Latin.

Wherever the Spanish settled they took power. They thought they were better than the Indians. Unlike the hard-working English settlers in North America, most Spanish settlers came from wealthy families. They felt "above" doing hard work themselves. So they made the Indians work for them. They also brought Africans to the New World to work as slaves on farms and in mines.

Many wealthy Spaniards lived on **haciendas**. These were large cattle ranches with rich farmlands. Work on the haciendas was done by Indian field hands or by African slaves.

Latin America Is Late to Industrialize

Spain and Portugal controlled all trade in their colonies. The colonies were not allowed to trade among themselves or with other nations. They were prevented from becoming less dependent on the mother country. And any effort to develop industry in the New World was crushed. Latin America had to sell all its raw materials to Spain and Portugal. And it had to buy all its finished products from them, too.

This kind of control kept industry from developing in Latin America. Eventually the people of Latin America rose up against their foreign rulers. The 1800s saw waves of revolution sweep through Latin America.

Social Classes in the Colonies

The people who had been born in Spain felt superior to the other Latin Americans. They did not adopt any native customs. Instead, the Spaniards tried to make the new land as much like Spain as possible.

The Creoles were people of Spanish blood who were born and raised in Latin America. Many Creoles resented the haughty attitude of the Spanish-born people. The Creoles would play a large part in the soon-to-come struggles for independence.

Most of the Spaniards and Portuguese who settled in Latin America did not bring their families. Many were soldiers and fortune-seekers. They did not plan to stay any longer than it took to get rich. Some fathered the children of native women. Over time there came to be a large class of people of mixed race. They were called "mestizos."

Many of the mestizos were angered by their lack of social standing. They hated the **discrimination** they felt from their Spanish rulers. The mestizos were ready for freedom from European rule.

The Indians and the African slaves were certainly ready for a change of government. Year after year, they worked hard and remained poor. They had nothing for themselves under European rule—no land, no wealth, no power, no hope.

The poor people of Latin America were now ready to fight for freedom. They saw North America's colonies win freedom from the English. They saw the French rise up against tyranny. Now they needed leaders to call them together and organize revolts.

Toussaint L'Ouverture

Haiti covers the western third of the island of Hispaniola in the Carribean Sea. It was the first Latin American country to fight for freedom. Haiti was a French colony. When news of revolution in France reached Haiti, the people of the colony got excited. They began to think about freedom, too.

In 1791 the slaves rebelled against their French masters. A black revolutionist named Toussaint L'Ouverture became a leader in Haiti's fight for freedom. Toussaint, a son of slaves, was a slave himself until he was 50. He led the slave revolt until 1793, when France freed all the slaves. In 1801 Toussaint became governor of Haiti. The very next year, however, Napoleon sent a French army to Haiti. He planned to reestablish slavery in the country. War broke out again. The French threw Toussaint into prison, where he died in 1803. But by 1804, the French army was defeated, and French rule in Haiti ended. Haiti declared its independence.

Wars of revolution continued. Other Latin American countries demanded freedom.

Toussaint L'Ouverture

Hidalgo and Morelos

Miguel Hidalgo and José Morelos led Mexico's revolt against Spain. Both men were Catholic priests. They organized the Indians in a revolution.

On September 16, 1810, in the town of Dolores, Miguel Hidalgo rang his church bells. He shouted the *grito de Dolores,* or "cry of Dolores": "Long live independence! Down with bad government!"

Both Hidalgo and Morelos lost their lives fighting for Mexico's independence. But by 1821, the fight was won. Now Mexico celebrates September 16th as its independence day. And the town of Dolores is now called Dolores Hidalgo.

Simón Bolívar

Simón Bolívar

Perhaps the best-known Latin American liberator was Simón Bolívar. Today he is called "The **Liberator**" and the "George Washington of South America."

Bolívar spent much of his life fighting for the independence of South American nations. He was a Creole, born in Venezuela. His parents were wealthy Spaniards. To keep his wealth and social position, Bolívar might have sided with Spain. But he believed in freedom from European rule. He spent all his money backing revolutions.

Starting in 1810, Simón Bolívar helped to organize an army. He then led the army to a series of victories against the Spanish. He liberated one country after another. At one time he ruled the newly formed republic of Gran Colombia. This was made up of Colombia, Venezuela, Ecuador, Panama, and Peru. Then Upper Peru became a separate state. In 1825 it was named Bolivia, in Bolívar's honor. Then, one by one, each country withdrew from the union. By 1828 Bolívar ruled only Colombia. His own people did not appreciate him. After a failed assassination attempt, he resigned as president in 1830. Bolívar died alone and poor. It was not until his death that he became honored as South America's liberator.

Bernardo O'Higgins

The country of Chile owes its liberation to the son of an Irishman. Bernardo O'Higgins's father had been a **viceroy** of Peru. Bernardo O'Higgins led a revolution that began in 1810. After winning Chile's independence from Spain in 1818, O'Higgins acted as the country's dictator. He planned to bring about reform in Chile. He taxed the wealthy landowners to pay for new schools and roads. And he tried to break up their big estates. But a revolt by the landowners in 1823 sent O'Higgins into exile.

José de San Martín

Bernardo O'Higgins was helped in his struggle against Spain by another great leader, José de San Martín. San Martín was born in Argentina, but was educated in Spain. While in Spain, he fought with the Spanish army against Napoleon. When he returned to Argentina, the fight for independence had already begun in South America.

In 1812 San Martín took command of a rebel army. For the next several years he fought to free his country from Spain's rule. In 1816 Argentina declared its independence. Then San Martín decided to help the rest of South America become free. He planned a daring surprise attack against the Spanish army in Chile. In 1817 he joined forces with Bernardo O'Higgins. Together, they led their army across the Andes Mountains. It was a difficult and dangerous march. Blizzards struck without warning. The men had to plow through deep snow drifts. Slowly they made their way across the icy mountain passes. Many men died along the way. Finally the brave leaders and their army came down from the mountains in Chile. There they attacked the Spanish army. The Spaniards were completely taken by surprise, and they were easily defeated.

San Martín then went on to help with independence for Peru in 1821. When he finally returned to Argentina, a fierce struggle for political power was going on. San Martín felt bad about this and would have nothing to do with it. He went back to Europe and for the rest of his life lived in France.

Dom Pedro

Dom Pedro led Brazil to independence without bloodshed. He was a Portuguese born in Rio de Janeiro, Brazil. He inherited the Brazilian kingdom when it was still under Portuguese rule.

Brazilians, like other South Americans, were asking for independence from European control. Dom Pedro was in favor of independence, too. The Portuguese in Europe called for Dom Pedro's return to Portugal. But Dom Pedro would not leave his home.

"I remain!" he stated. And on September 7, 1822, he declared Brazil an independent country. He took the throne of the newly independent nation as Pedro I.

Governments of the New Nations

The Latin American countries' struggles for independence did not necessarily mean freedom for the people. Most of the countries did not become democracies. So life did not change much for poor Indians.

Heading for the market place in Chinchero, Peru

Dictators ruled most of the new nations. These dictators were powerful men with strong armies behind them. Any changes in government usually came only by military takeovers.

Latin American Cultures

Latin American culture is really more than one culture. It is a mixture of several different peoples: Indian, Spanish, Portuguese, African, and French.

Some of the Indians still live much like their ancestors. They wear woven shawls and take their goods to market along mountain roads on **burros**. They play music on handmade wooden instruments and weave baskets of cane and reed. Indian women still spin and weave colorful cloth. There is often a note of sadness to the Indians' art. A **mural** in Mexico City shows the Indians suffering at the hands of Spanish conquistadors.

The Spanish and Portuguese brought their languages and religion to Latin America. Most of the people of Latin America speak Spanish. Portuguese is the main language of Brazil. And the different Indian tribes speak their own native languages. Roman Catholicism is the main religion.

Spanish architecture is common in Latin America. Many homes, churches, and public buildings have a Spanish flavor. But much Latin American music reflects the music of Africa. The Africans brought their songs and dances with them when they came to Latin America as slaves.

Typical Spanish colonial architecture, Taxco, Mexico

Different races and cultures **dominate** different areas of Latin America. In some countries, most of the people are Indians. The art, music, dress, and customs in Guatemala, Bolivia, and Peru are Indian. And in some countries, like Haiti, the people are mostly **descendants** of Africans.

Latin America gets its name from of the colonization and **influence** of Latin peoples—the Spanish, the Portuguese, and the French. But the Indians and the Africans also played a large part in making the land what it is today.

Latin American nations become independent

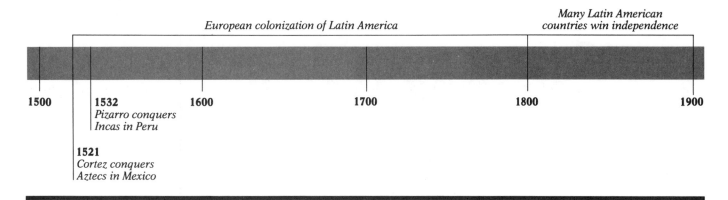

European colonization of Latin America

Many Latin American countries win independence

1500

1532
Pizarro conquers Incas in Peru

1600

1700

1800

1900

1521
Cortez conquers Aztecs in Mexico

Points to Remember

♦ Most areas of Latin America were settled by the Spanish and the Portuguese.

♦ The European settlers made workers of the Indians and brought slaves to Latin America from Africa.

♦ Mother countries did not allow industry to develop in Latin America.

♦ The various populations of Latin America, between 1500 and 1900, consisted of Europeans, Creoles, mestizos, Indians, and African slaves.

♦ The 1800s brought revolutions of independence to Latin America.

♦ By the end of the 1800s, there were many independent Latin American countries.

♦ The governments of the independent countries were often run by dictators.

♦ Latin American culture is a blend of Spanish, Portuguese, French, Indian, and African cultures.

Think About It!

1. How did slavery play a part in Latin America?

2. How did the French and American revolutions encourage revolution in Latin America?

3. How did Spanish settlers in Latin America treat the Indians? The Creoles? The mestizos?

4. In what ways were the Europeans who settled in Latin America different from the colonists in North America?

5. Why would the United States have been disappointed with many of the governments that developed in the independent Latin American nations?

6. Why would there be a "note of sadness" to much of the Indian art?

Chapter 6

The Changing World: North America

Words to Know	**sympathy** feeling sorry for another's suffering	**victor** the winner of a battle, war, struggle, or contest
reaper a machine for cutting down and gathering grain crops	**territory** the land ruled by a nation or state	

Look for the answers as you read:

1. How did the Monroe Doctrine affect European imperialism in North and South America?

2. How did the United States gain the Louisiana Territory?

3. What problems did the United States face in establishing its northern and southern borders? How were these problems solved?

4. What happened to United States industry after the Civil War?

5. How did the United States acquire Alaska? Hawaii?

6. How did the Spanish-American war result in more power for the United States and make the United States a more imperialistic nation?

Smaller nations are often threatened by larger and stronger nations. The new, independent countries in Latin America struggled to survive. The United States wanted these countries to remain independent.

In 1823 James Monroe, president of the United States, spoke before his Congress. He said that the United States would not allow Europe to set up new colonies in North or South America. Nor would it allow any existing colonies to take over more land. The president's statement against European imperialism is called the Monroe Doctrine.

Imperialism and the Monroe Doctrine

The United States grew rapidly during the early 1800s. Settlers moved west, taking lands from the Indians.

In 1803 Thomas Jefferson was president of the United States. He arranged for the United States to buy a large piece of land from France. This treaty was called the Louisiana Purchase. The United States paid about $15 million for 828,000 square miles of land. This land, the Louisiana **Territory**, almost doubled the size of the United States.

American pioneers streamed into the new land. They settled first in what would become the states of Louisiana, Arkansas, and Missouri.

A Growing United States: The Louisiana Purchase

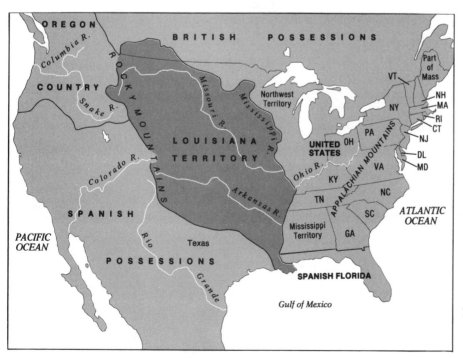

The Louisiana Purchase, 1803

United States Borders

The United States needed to set up clear northern and southern borders. England still controlled Canada, to the north. War broke out between England and the United States in 1812. But the border had never been in question. Other problems had led to the war. England had been interfering with United States trade. A peace treaty was signed in December of 1814. The border remained the same as it had been before. In the southern United States, however, border disagreements *were* the cause of war.

What is now the state of Texas once belonged to the Republic of Mexico. But many settlers from the United States moved into Texas. The Mexicans worried about the large numbers of settlers from the North. They said that no more settlers could come in from the United States. So the settlers rebelled. In November 1835 they declared themselves free from Mexico. Then the battles began.

"Remember the Alamo!"

The Battle of the Alamo was one of the most famous battles in the Texan war for independence. The Alamo was an old Spanish mission the Texans were using as their fort.

On February 23, 1836, 5,000 Mexican soldiers stormed the fort. Inside the Alamo were 187 Texans, among them Davy Crockett and James Bowie. They managed to hold the fort for 12 days. In the end, every American defending the Alamo was killed. But their brave fight gave spirit to the Texans' struggle and helped to win the war.

"Remember the Alamo!" became the battle cry of the United States forces. By April 1836 the Mexican army was defeated. The Mexican general Santa Anna signed a peace treaty.

The Battle of the Alamo

In 1845 Texas became the 28th state to join the United States. The Mexican government had never actually agreed to Texas's independence. So the declaration of statehood led to war in 1846 between the United States and Mexico.

Mexico lost the war in 1848. The United States gained vast new territory that had belonged to Mexico. This included California, Nevada, Utah, Arizona, and parts of New Mexico and Colorado. Now Mexico accused Americans of imperialism. The United States was charged with taking over foreign lands and ruling them.

War with Mexico

Like European history, American history is scarred with many wars. Between 1861 and 1865, Americans fought a bloody civil war between the northern and southern states.

While slavery was an issue, it was not the cause of the war. After Abraham Lincoln became president, the southern states broke away from the United States. They formed a separate nation called the Confederate States of America. Lincoln could not allow the South to break up the union. He felt he had no choice but to go to war.

The North had many more people than the South. And the North had more manufacturing and industry. It was able to produce more guns and cannons. The South was still mainly agricultural. Its main crops were cotton and tobacco. And the southern plantations depended on slave labor.

Northerners expected the war to be over soon. And they were sure they would be the winners. But they were in for a surprise. The very first battle of the war, at Bull Run on April 21, 1861, was easily won by the South! And the Confederate army went on to win one battle after another. The army was led by brilliant generals such as Robert E. Lee and Stonewall Jackson.

Then Ulysses S. Grant took command of the northern armies. The tides of battle turned. The North finally began to get the upper hand. In 1863 Lincoln signed the Emancipation Proclamation, outlawing slavery. Blacks were invited to join the northern forces. By the end of the war, about 200,000 blacks had fought for the North.

By 1865 much of the South lay in ruins. And the southern armies had become much weaker. Little by little, the North had cut off all of the South's supply routes. Lee's army was trapped in Virginia by Grant's army. Lee decided it was hopeless to keep on fighting. He surrendered to Grant on April 9, 1865, at Appomattox Court House.

The bloodiest war in American history was over. More than 600,000 people had been killed. Many cities and farms had been destroyed. But the North had won the war. And all of the states remained united.

America's Civil War

Industry in the United States

Many changes occurred in the United States during the early 1800s. The introduction of the steam locomotive led to great improvements in overland transportation. And Samuel Morse's telegraph, first demonstrated in 1837, led to greatly improved communication. In 1834 Cyrus McCormick invented a mechanical **reaper**. This machine allowed farmers to harvest grain much more quickly than before. And beginning in the early 1800s, some businesses began building factories. Inside the factories were machines that enabled workers to produce goods more rapidly.

After the Civil War, changes occurred faster. More and more factories were built. And machines began to replace hand labor as the main means of manufacturing. At this time, a new nationwide network of railroads was being built. In 1869 the transcontinental railroad was completed. This linked up the eastern and western parts of the country. And it helped speed up the settlement of the West.

The railroad system helped businesses to distribute their goods more quickly. And there were more and more goods available. Inventors developed new products. And businesses were able to make the products in large quantities. The United States now had its own industrial revolution.

Many big businesses grew up during this period. They included coal mining, petroleum, steel, and industrial machinery. New England, New York, and Pennsylvania became important industrial centers in the North. The United States was on its way to becoming an industrial giant.

Further Expansion: Alaska and Hawaii

"A foolish purchase!" "Who wants a hunk of frozen land?" That is what many Americans said about the territory known as Alaska. In 1867 Secretary of State William Seward had persuaded the United States to buy Alaska from Russia. It cost just over $7 million. But in 1897, gold was discovered there. It was only then that Americans began to realize the value of the purchase.

Americans' interest in Hawaii began in 1820. That year a group of Protestant missionaries from New England arrived there. In 1835 the first sugar plantation began operating. It was owned by an American company. Commercial development of the pineapple began in the mid-1800s. Also, around this time, hundreds of American whaling ships began to visit Hawaii regularly. In 1887 the United States signed a treaty with Hawaii. It gave the United States the right to use Pearl Harbor as a naval base. United States presence and interests were now well-established on the islands.

American naval officers being entertained at a feast, Hawaii

In 1893 the Hawaiians staged a revolution against Liliuokalani, queen of Hawaii. Americans, who by that time owned most of Hawaii's industry, encouraged and led the revolt. Queen Liliuokalani left her throne. In 1900 Hawaii became a territory of the United States.

The United States used the Monroe Doctrine to keep European interests out of the Americas. Meanwhile the United States gained more and more territory for itself.

The Spanish-American War

A war broke out between the United States and Spain in 1898. This resulted in the United States gaining still more territory.

The United States wanted Spain out of the Caribbean area. Many Americans felt **sympathy** for the Cubans who lived under harsh Spanish rule. And some Americans saw a chance for the United States to gain more power.

Relations between the United States and Spain were tense. Then, in February of 1898, the U.S. battleship *Maine* exploded in the harbor at Havana, Cuba. Many Americans blamed Spain. By April the Spanish-American War had begun.

By August of that same year, the war was over. The United States was the **victor**. In December, Spain and the United States sent representatives to Paris to sign a treaty. The Treaty of Paris gave the United States possession of Puerto Rico, the Philippines, and the Pacific island of Guam. Spain gave Cuba its freedom.

U.S. Power

By the early 1900s, the United States was the strongest country on the American continents. It held control over lands gained in the Spanish-American War. During that war, the U.S. Navy sent a battleship from San Francisco to Cuba. It had to sail all the way around the tip of South America. This is a distance of 13,000 miles. If there had been a canal across Central America, the trip would have been only 4,600 miles.

U.S. president Theodore Roosevelt wanted to build such a canal across Panama. But Colombia ruled Panama. And Colombia would not grant the United States the land it needed for the canal. So Americans encouraged Panamanians to declare their independence from Colombia.

Panama's rebellion in November of 1903 was a success. The United States gained the right to build its canal. Panama sold the United States a "canal zone" ten miles wide. The Panama Canal and the Canal Zone belonged to the United States. But in 1977, the United States and Panama signed a treaty. In keeping with the treaty, Panama regained control of the Canal Zone in 1979. And in 1999, Panama is to gain control of the canal itself.

But with the canal built, the United States grew as an economic, military, and industrial power. And the United States took its place as a major force in the history of the modern world.

Building the Panama Canal

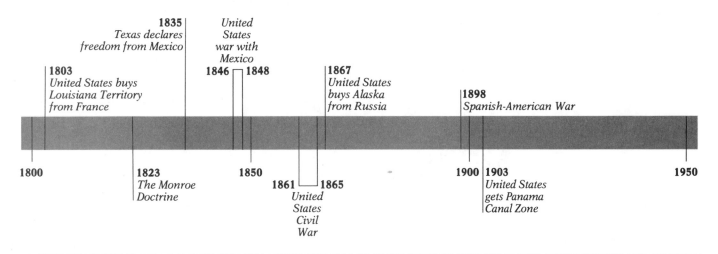

1835
Texas declares freedom from Mexico

United States war with Mexico
1846 — **1848**

1803
United States buys Louisiana Territory from France

1867
United States buys Alaska from Russia

1898
Spanish-American War

1800

1823
The Monroe Doctrine

1850

1861 — **1865**
United States Civil War

1900 | **1903**
United States gets Panama Canal Zone

1950

Points to Remember

♦ The Monroe Doctrine said that the United States would not allow Europeans to set up colonies in the Americas.

♦ The United States expanded by adding the Louisiana Territory, Alaska, and Hawaii.

♦ War with Mexico established the southern border of the United States.

♦ The United States was torn apart by a bloody civil war from 1861 to 1865.

♦ The United States became a more industrialized nation after the Civil War.

♦ The Spanish-American War gave the United States Puerto Rico, the Philippines, and Guam.

♦ The United States had become an imperialistic nation itself.

Think About It!

1. What is imperialism?

2. What does the phrase "Remember the Alamo" refer to?

3. What did Americans think about the purchase of Alaska?

4. What events could lead people to call the United States an imperialistic country?

5. Why might some countries object to the way the United States got the Panama Canal?

Chapter 7

The Changing World: The Far East

Words to Know

addicted having a strong habit that is hard to give up

impressed affected thoughts and feelings

interference meddling in another's affairs without being asked

international having to do with many nations

modern of the present time, up-to-date

policies rules, methods of action or conduct

smuggled moved something into or out of a country secretly because it is against the law

sought looked for, searched for

Look for the answers as you read:

1. How did Manchu rulers look upon the other Chinese?

2. What was the Opium War, and what did it cost China?

3. What was the Open-Door Policy?

4. How did Sun Yat-sen put an end to Manchu rule?

5. How did Commodore Matthew C. Perry open the doors of trade to Japan?

6. What happened to Japanese feudalism, shoguns, and samurai?

7. In what ways did Japan modernize after a powerful emperor took over in 1867?

8. How did Japan's industrialization lead to Japanese imperialism?

The Manchus Establish the Ch'ing Dynasty in China

Manchuria is a region in the northeastern part of China. At one time, it did not belong to China. In 1644 the Manchus—the people of Manchuria—invaded northern China. They overthrew the Ming dynasty that was then in power. Then they conquered the rest of China. The Manchus set up their own dynasty called the Ch'ing dynasty. The Manchus would remain in power for more than 250 years. And the Ch'ing dynasty would be the last of the Chinese dynasties.

The Manchus were a proud people—too proud, perhaps. They thought they were better than the other Chinese people. They passed a law saying that a Manchu could not marry a Chinese. They forced Chinese men to wear a Manchu hairstyle. This was a long braid down the back of the head. The British later called the long braid a "queue." This word means "tail" in Latin.

China under the Ch'ing dynasty

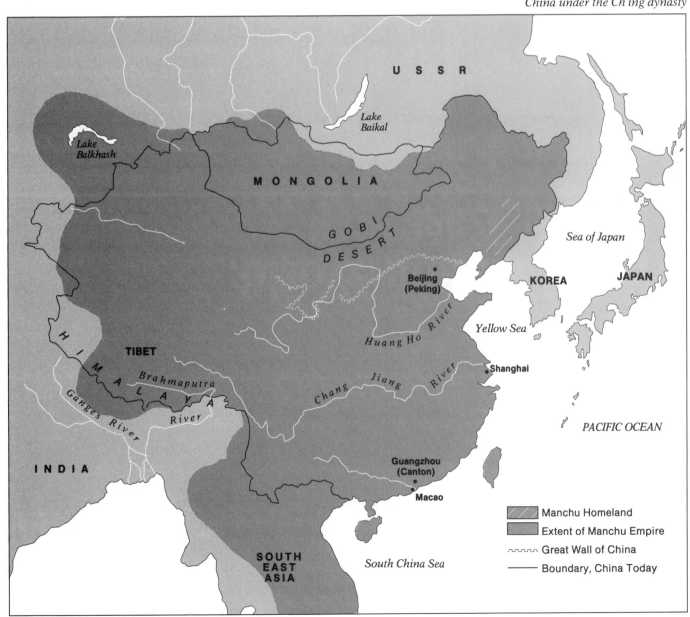

Manchu Homeland
Extent of Manchu Empire
Great Wall of China
Boundary, China Today

The Manchus not only looked down on other Chinese, they looked down on the rest of the world. Until the mid-1800s, foreign trade was allowed through only one Chinese city—Canton. When European nations and America asked for more trade with China, the Manchu rulers always refused.

During the first 150 years of Manchu rule, China enjoyed prosperity. Agriculture increased, and the handicraft industry did, too. The population expanded rapidly. But by the late 1700s, the times had changed. The population had increased faster than the food supply. Life became harder for most people.

China also suffered because of the Manchus' isolationist policies. Once China had been a leader in science and medicine. But by the 1800s, the Chinese had fallen behind the Europeans in all areas of science and invention. From this point on, the Manchus would rule a troubled China.

Chinese men with hair braided in queue

The Opium Wars

Europeans wanted tea and silk from China. And they wanted a new source of raw materials.

"But there is nothing we want from you in return," the Manchus told the Europeans. "Why should we allow trade?"

Then the Europeans found something the Chinese did want. They found opium.

Opium is a dangerous drug made from the seeds of a poppy. The poppies grew in India. European merchants began to bring opium to China during the early 1800s. Many Chinese became **addicted** to the drug. So China passed a law making opium trade illegal. But the demand for opium was still there. Now the Europeans **smuggled** the drug into China, making large profits.

In 1839 a Manchu official seized 20,000 chests of opium from British merchants in Canton. He had the opium burned. The British were angry. Valuable property had been destroyed. Great Britain went to war with China, demanding better trading rights. China had little chance against Britain's armies. In 1842 the Chinese surrendered. They signed the Treaty of Nan-ching.

This was the first of what the Chinese called the "Unequal Treaties." China not only had to pay for the lost opium but for the cost of the war. China had to open five ports to British trade. And China gave the island of Hong Kong to Great Britain. Also, the new treaties totally protected British merchants from Chinese law. No Englishman could be tried for any crime in a Chinese court—even if the crime were committed in China. The Chinese felt helpless.

Chinese Rebellion

The Manchus had trouble with foreigners and trouble with their own people. Chinese farmers were not happy under Manchu rule. They said that the rulers were greedy and unfair. Most Chinese farmers were very poor. Finally the peasants rebelled. They called their rebellion "Taiping," meaning "Great Peace." The Taiping Rebellion lasted from 1851 to 1864. Millions of lives were lost. When it was over, the Manchus still ruled China.

The peasants might have won their fight. They might have overthrown the Manchu government. But foreign **interference** worked against them. Foreign governments wanted to keep the Manchus in power. They worried that they might lose their trade rights if the Manchus were overthrown. So the British supported the Manchus throughout the Taiping Rebellion. They sent military help, and the peasants were defeated.

War with Japan

Next the Manchus faced war with Japan.

China had had claims on Korea for hundreds of years. When a rebellion broke out in Korea in 1894, the Chinese sent troops in to crush it. Japan had interests in Korea, too. So it sent in its own troops. The rebellion was put down. But neither Japan nor China would withdraw troops. Instead, the two countries began fighting each other.

By April of 1895, the Japanese had defeated the Chinese. China had to give up much of its claim on Korea. China also had to give the island of Taiwan to the Japanese. In 1910 Japan took complete control of Korea.

The Chinese-Japanese war left China weak. From then on Manchu rulers commanded little respect.

The Open-Door Policy

By 1899 China feared that European nations might step in and divide the land into colonies. The United States suggested an Open-Door Policy. This meant that all countries would have equal rights to trade in China. China agreed to this policy. The Chinese had once kept everyone out. Now they opened their ports to the world.

A Manchu Empress and the Boxer Rebellion

In 1898 the empress T'zu Hsi ruled the Ch'ing dynasty. She was very old-fashioned. She wanted to stop any change in China. Perhaps she remembered China's glorious past. If she had her way, she would keep China the way it was.

Then something happened in 1900, during the empress's reign. A group of Chinese rebelled against all foreigners in China. The revolt was called the Boxer Rebellion. And the empress T'zu Hsi secretly supported the rebels.

The Boxers were members of a secret society. Westerners called them "Boxers" because they practiced Chinese exercises that resembled shadow-boxing. The Boxers attempted to kill all foreigners in China. They were put down by an **international** army that included soldiers from the United States.

China was forced to make payments to the foreign countries to make up for the rebellion. The United States used much of the money it received to educate Chinese students. Because of this the United States won China's favor.

American troops in Beijing during the Boxer Rebellion

The Last Dynasty

The Manchus would rule the last Chinese dynasty. And the Ch'ing dynasty was nearly at its end. Rebellions had weakened the government. The war with Japan had cost China both land and power. Many foreign countries had interests in China now. And the weak Manchus were unable to protect China against the foreigners.

China needed a new government if it were to survive.

Sun Yat-sen and the Chinese Nationalists

Dr. Sun Yat-sen would lead a revolution in China. Born in China, Sun Yat-sen had been educated in London. Although he lived outside of China, he remained loyal to his homeland.

In 1911 Sun Yat-sen was in Denver, Colorado. When he heard about sparks of revolution in China, he returned there. He led the revolution and overthrew the Manchu empire. On January 1, 1912, he became the first president of China's new republic. The last Manchu emperor, Pu-Yi, gave up the throne on February 12, 1912. He was only six years old at the time.

Sun's term as president was short, less than two months. Then a strong, northern Chinese group took over. They put a dictator in charge and exiled Sun Yat-sen.

But Sun's followers remained. They organized the *Kuomintang*, or Nationalist party. For ten years the Chinese people suffered under harsh rulers who fought each other for power.

Then Sun Yat-sen returned and set up a rival government in Canton. By 1922 the republic had failed and civil war was widespread. With the support of the Soviet Union and Chinese communists, Sun and his Nationalist party trained an army. They set out to bring China together under a Nationalist government.

Sun Yat-sen died in 1925, but his work was finished by Chiang Kai-shek. By 1928 Chiang was able to set up a Nationalist government in China.

More days of war and revolution were ahead. But China had left its great dynasties behind and moved into the modern world.

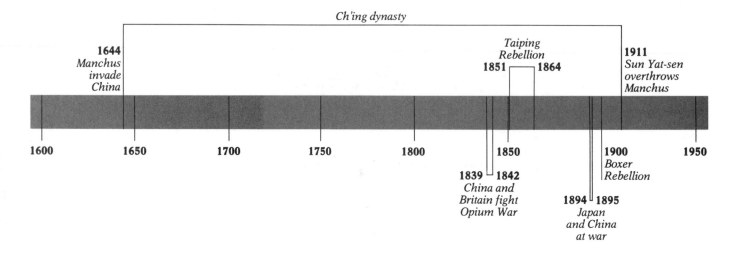

Japan Opens Its Doors

Since 1600 Japan had been an isolated nation. The whole country was under the rule of the Tokugawa family. All foreign trade and travel were forbidden. Japan had not allowed foreign products to enter its ports. Nor did it send any products to other lands. Japan would not accept visitors from other countries. In fact, if a foreign seaman were shipwrecked on Japan's shores, he was in for trouble. He could be arrested or even killed.

In 1853 an American naval officer, Commodore Matthew C. Perry, changed all that. Commodore Perry sailed four U.S. warships into Tokyo Bay. He brought a letter from U.S. president Franklin Pierce. The letter asked the Japanese to change their **policies**. It asked for better treatment of any shipwrecked American sailors. It asked that American whaling ships be allowed to buy supplies at Japanese ports. It asked that Japan agree to trade with the United States.

The Japanese were **impressed** by Perry and his United States ships. They had never seen such large vessels or such mighty guns. Perry was a stern man. He met the Japanese with dignity. He refused to speak to anyone except the highest officials. Perry left his requests for the Japanese to consider.

The next year Commodore Perry returned to Japan. This time he brought even more ships. The ruling shogun spoke with Perry. Then the Japanese ruler signed a treaty with the United States. Japanese ports would be open to United States ships. It was the beginning of a new Japan.

Commodore Matthew Perry

Commodore Perry's procession through the streets of Yokohama

In 1858 Townsend Harris, a U.S. diplomat, signed a more extensive treaty with Japan. That same year Japan signed trade treaties with Great Britain, France, the Netherlands, and Russia. Japan was no longer an isolated nation.

Then came years of change. Japan was torn between its old ways and the new. Some Japanese wanted to drive the foreigners out of Japan again. They said the treaties Japan had signed were "unequal treaties." Others wanted to accept the western world, to learn what they could.

The Japanese had met the **modern** world. And they realized that their feudal system of government was outdated. The rule of the shoguns with their samurai warriors had to end.

A Modern Japan

In 1867 a young emperor took over as the power behind Japan. The emperor and his followers began to modernize the country. Their motto was, "Knowledge shall be **sought** throughout the world." The emperor adopted *Meiji* as his title, which means "enlightened rule." He was to rule Japan until 1912. These years are known as the Meiji period. The Japanese traveled to other nations. They wanted to learn what they could about industry, education, transportation, and banking. They built thousands of schools. And they invited foreigners to teach in Japan.

In 1889 Japan's first constitution was written. The emperor, whom the Japanese considered divine, still held the power. But he accepted advice from elected representatives.

By the 1890s Japan was keeping step with the modern world. Japan had done away with the samurai and now had a modern army and navy. Japan had steel mills and shipyards and electrical power plants. In just over 25 years, Japan had made amazing progress. It had gone from an isolated, feudal nation to become one of the world's industrial powers.

Imperialism and Japan

As industry grew, Japan needed more raw materials. Like many strong nations, Japan decided to set up overseas colonies to supply those raw materials. But gaining such colonies meant war.

From 1894 to 1895, Japan was at war with China. China and Japan had conflicting claims in Korea. Japan, with its new, modern military, easily defeated China.

In 1904 Russia tried to stake claims in Korea. Japan declared war. The Russo-Japanese War was costly to both sides. But in 1905 the war was over. Again the Japanese were the victors. Japan took over some lands in China that had been controlled by Russia. And in 1910, Japan took complete control of Korea. Japan's victory over Russia surprised the world. For the first time, an Asian nation had proved to be stronger than a European nation. And this was to be only the first chapter in the story of Japanese imperialism.

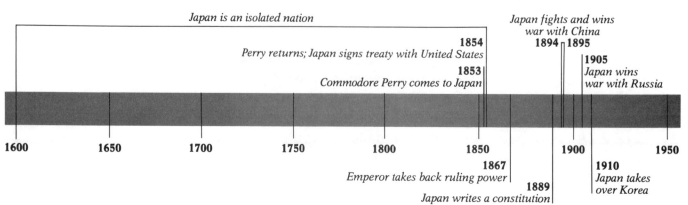

Points to Remember

◆ The Manchus conquered China in 1644 and established the Ch'ing dynasty.

◆ The Manchus looked down on other Chinese and on Europeans.

◆ The Manchus tried to limit foreign trade in China.

◆ China and Britain fought a war after China destroyed an illegal British opium cargo.

◆ Chinese peasants rebelled in the Taiping Rebellion in 1851. But they were put down by the Manchus and British by 1864.

◆ The United States persuaded China to have an "open-door policy" toward foreign trade.

◆ In 1900 the Boxers tried to drive foreigners out of China. But the Boxer Rebellion was crushed by foreign armies.

◆ The Manchus were overthrown in 1911 by Chinese Nationalists led by Dr. Sun Yat-sen. That was the end of dynasty rule in China.

◆ In 1853 Commodore Perry sailed into Tokyo Bay and negotiated treaties with Japan.

◆ Soon after the Japanese began trade with the United States, they opened their doors to other countries.

◆ In 1867 a young emperor took over the rule of Japan from the shoguns. Japan's feudal days were over.

◆ Japan became a powerful industrial nation in just over 25 years.

◆ Japan built a strong, modern military.

◆ When new industry led to a need for raw materials, Japan became imperialistic.

◆ Japan won new lands in wars with China in 1894 to 1895 and with Russia in 1904 to 1905.

Think About It!

1. Why did the Chinese fear European imperialism?

2. What were the weaknesses of the Manchu rule?

3. Why do you think the Chinese called treaties made after the Opium War "unequal treaties"?

4. Why did the Boxers rebel?

5. How did the United States Navy's Commodore Matthew C. Perry open the doors of trade to Japan?

6. What happened to Japanese feudalism, shoguns, and samurai?

7. In what ways did Japan modernize after a powerful emperor took over in 1867?

8. How did Japan's industrialization lead to Japanese imperialism?

9. What did Japan win in the wars with China and Russia?

Chapter 8

The Changing World: India

Look for the answers as you read:

1. Why did Mogul power weaken after Aurangzeb's reign as emperor?

2. How did the British East India Company come to indirectly rule India?

3. How did the sepoy rebellion begin? How did it lead to direct British rule?

4. What good things did Britain do for India?

5. Why were many Indians unhappy with British rule?

6. Who was Mahatma Gandhi, and what was different about his way of revolution?

Aurangzeb, the last powerful Mogul emperor, died in 1707. The Moguls had ruled India for almost 200 years. Aurangzeb, a Moslem, had been a harsh ruler. He had angered the Hindus by destroying many of their temples. He had tried to force non-Moslems to convert to Islam.

After the death of Aurangzeb, the Mogul Empire began to break up. Once again, India was divided into small kingdoms. The rajas of the different kingdoms quarreled. The Mogul rulers no longer had any real power.

As the Moguls weakened, stronger countries saw their chance. Europeans would take advantage of the unsteady government in India.

The Fall of the Mogul Empire

Trading between Europe and India had been going on for a long time. In 1498 the Portuguese explorer Vasco da Gama reached India by sailing around Africa. From that time on, European merchants made regular voyages to India. Dutch, Portuguese, French, and English traders fought each other for control of Indian trade.

In 1600 a private business called the British East India Company was formed. Its purpose was to trade with India. It set up trading posts along India's coastline at Bombay, Calcutta, and Madras. At around this time, the Dutch East India Company was formed. It began operating out of Java, in Indonesia.

The Europeans gained little in India as long as the Mogul Empire was strong. But by the mid-1700s, there was no longer a strong central government in India. The British East India Company became very involved in what went on in that country. It took sides in Indian civil wars. And it supported rulers who gave it favorable trade rights.

When the French began the French East India Company, the British went to war with them. In 1757 an Englishman named Robert Clive led the British to victory against the French. Both Clive's army and the French army used Indian soldiers to fight their war. The Indian soldiers were called "sepoys." The British drove the French out of India. And the British East India Company became a powerful force in India.

The British East India Company

The East India Company Rules

Soon **agents** of the East India Company became stronger than the local rajas. By 1850 the British agents controlled more than half of the land in India. The British put their own men into all the important positions. Englishmen led sepoy armies. They became wealthy landholders.

The British **imposed** their own ways on the Indian society. They built Christian churches and spoke out against the Hindu caste system. Many of the Indians did not like the English ways. And they did not like the East India Company, either.

For almost 100 years, Britain **indirectly** ruled India through its East India Company. India was not officially a British colony. But the British held all the power.

The Sepoy Rebellion

To protect their own power, the East India agents from Britain built up armies of sepoys. Most of the British army officers never tried to understand Indian customs and culture. They insisted that the Indians accept British ways.

The sepoys grumbled about this. Then in 1857, the British started using a new kind of bullet in India. To open the **cartridge**, a soldier had to bite off its end. The new cartridges were greased with the fat from cows and pigs. The Moslem religion forbids its followers to eat pork. Hindus are not allowed to eat the meat of a cow. So the sepoys refused to bite the bullets. When British officers ordered them to bite open the cartridges, the sepoys rebelled.

The British put down the sepoy rebellion in 1858. But many lives were lost. Britain saw that the East India Company could no longer be trusted with control of India.

The Sepoy Rebellion

British Rule

In 1858 the British parliament took over the rule of India. India became a colony of Great Britain. It was now called "British India," or the "British Raj."

A viceroy ran the colony. He was appointed by the British monarch. In 1877 the British held a splendid ceremony in India. On this occasion Queen Victoria was named empress of India.

The British profited from their Indian colony. They called India the "Jewel of the British Empire." In turn, the British government tried to treat Indians more fairly than the East India Company had.

Sahibgunge station near Calcutta, 1867

The British tried to solve the problems of poverty that had always troubled India. They helped farmers dig irrigation canals. They set up hospitals in cities and in some villages. They built railroads and factories and roads and schools. The British tried to do away with the harsh caste system that kept many people so poor.

But many Indians were unhappy. Some were poorer than ever. India's raw materials were all going to British industry. Manufactured goods were brought in from Britain, killing off India's own industries. Machine-made cloth poured in from Britain. This resulted in Indian spinners and weavers being put out of work. And all of India's top jobs went to the British.

It was clear to the Indians that the British looked down on them. The British did not allow Indians in their restaurants or hotels. To the people of India, it seemed that British imperialism encouraged British feelings of **superiority.**

Giant arch built by the British, Bombay

Ideas of Independence

The British chose some Indian students to send off to school in Great Britain. They planned to give the students "English" ideas and training. But the plan backfired. Once the students from India learned about English democracy, they wanted independence for their own people.

In 1885 a group called the Indian National Congress was founded. It was made up of educated Indians. They said they were meeting to improve relations with Britain. But in truth, they discussed revolution. In the early 1900s, there were some violent uprisings. The British always crushed them. To improve the situation, the British allowed a few Indians to be included in the government. A few years later, the British increased the number of Indians in the government. But protests continued.

Then on April 13, 1919, British troops fired on an unarmed crowd in Amritsar. Nearly 400 Indians were killed. And at least 1,200 were wounded. The Amritsar Massacre marked a turning point in British-Indian relations. From now on, Indians knew what they could expect from the British. They were determined to keep on fighting for independence.

But no real progress toward independence came until leadership went to a man named Gandhi.

Mahatma Gandhi

Mohandas K. Gandhi was born in 1869. He was a Hindu. His family belonged to the merchant caste. Gandhi studied law in London. He worked as a lawyer in South Africa for 21 years. At that time, South Africa was ruled by Great Britain. Gandhi worked for the rights of Indians, who were being discriminated against. In 1915 Gandhi returned to India. There he began to work for independence from Great Britain. In 1920 he became leader of the Indian National Congress.

Gandhi had new ideas about how to win independence. He taught that the way to freedom was not through violence or bloodshed. Gandhi believed in **nonviolent resistance**. He taught **civil disobedience**. Calmly and peacefully, he led Indians to refuse to obey the British government.

"Conquer by love," Gandhi taught. His followers called him "Mahatma" Gandhi. Mahatma means "Great Soul."

"We cannot win against British guns," Mahatma Gandhi said. "The British only know how to fight against guns. We will show them a new kind of resistance." Gandhi told his people that they had a weapon stronger than guns. That weapon was nonviolent disobedience. He told Indians to refuse to work in British mines, shops, and factories.

Mahatma Gandhi

Gandhi led a revolution for independence. It was, for the most part, a revolution of the poor. Although he was a Hindu, Gandhi did not believe in the caste system. He lived among the poorest Indians, the untouchables, for many years. He lived simply, often wearing only a linen **loincloth.**

In one act of resistance, Gandhi led thousands of Indian women to the train tracks. There they lay down, stopping the British trains. When the British put an unfair tax on salt, Gandhi did not answer the tax with violence. Instead, he peacefully led a march 200 miles to the sea to get salt from the ocean.

Gandhi was often arrested for his activities. He spent a total of seven years in jail. But in time, the British began to listen to Mahatma Gandhi and his followers.

Mahatma Gandhi and
followers on his "march to the sea"

Gandhi Insists on Peace

The British knew that the Indian people no longer wanted them in their country. They knew it was just a matter of time before they would be forced to leave. So the British offered independence to India. But the Moslems demanded a separate nation. They staged a protest that led to bloody rioting between Moslems and Hindus. As a result, India was divided into two nations. Pakistan would be a Moslem nation, and India would be Hindu.

Mahatma Gandhi saw his country gain independence in 1947. Unfortunately, more fighting between Hindus and Moslems came with independence. There was terrible loss of life. Entire villages were wiped out. Gandhi insisted that the fighting stop. He called for peace. He went on a **fast**, refusing to eat until the bloodshed ended. Gandhi almost starved to death. But at last, Hindu and Moslem leaders promised to stop their fighting. They did not want their great leader to die.

Gandhi's fast ended on June 30, 1948. Shortly after that, Gandhi was shot down by a Hindu gunman. Both Hindus and Moslems mourned their leader.

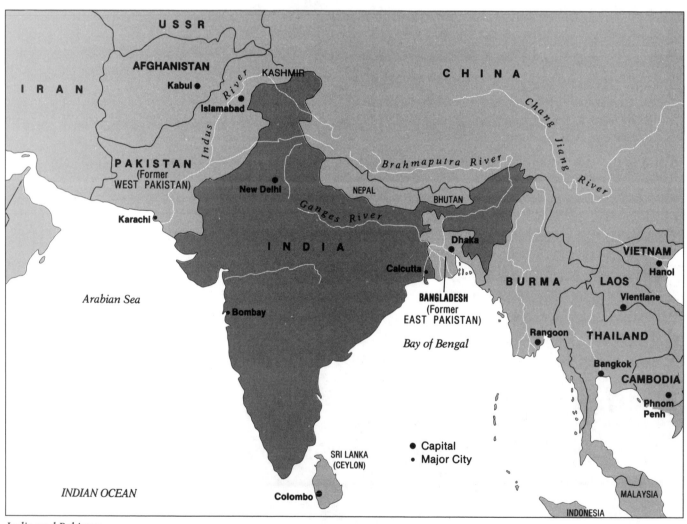

India and Pakistan

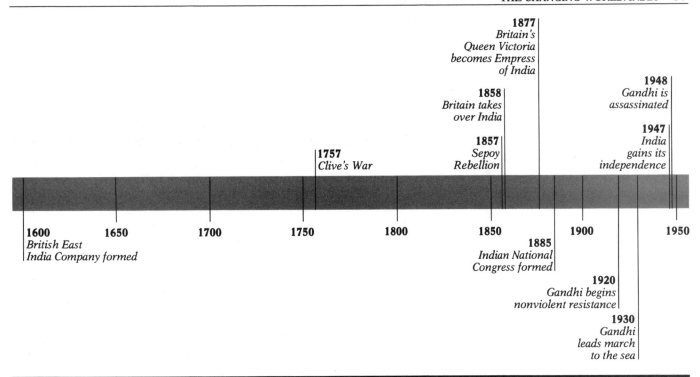

Points to Remember

◆ Mogul rule in India weakened in the early 1700s.

◆ The British East India Company, a private trading business, began to indirectly rule India.

◆ Indian soldiers, called "sepoys," rebelled against the East India Company in 1857.

◆ The British helped India progress, but kept themselves above the Indian population.

◆ A group of Indians, called the Indian National Congress, talked about independence from Great Britain.

◆ Mahatma Gandhi led India to independence by encouraging nonviolent civil disobedience.

◆ In 1947 India won independence and was divided into India and Pakistan.

Think About It!

1. What two religious groups fought each other throughout much of India's history? How was India divided between these groups after it gained independence?

2. Why did the Indian soldiers refuse to bite bullets greased with animal fat?

3. How did the English treat the Indians?

4. Describe Mahatma Gandhi's ways of revolution.

5. Do you know of any times in the United States when Gandhi's ideas have been used? If so, tell about them.

Chapter 9

The Changing World: Africa

Words to Know

caravans groups of people traveling together, often through a desert

conference a meeting of people to discuss something

dominance the act of ruling, controlling, being most powerful

inferior not as good as someone or something else

prejudice dislike of a people just because they are of a different race or religion, or are from another country

racism the idea that one race is better than another

staff a pole used for support in walking or to hold a flag

Look for the answers to these questions as you read:

1. What were the early kingdoms of western Africa?

2. How did Mali become a wealthy kingdom?

3. Why did Europe have little contact with Africa south of the Sahara Desert before the 1400s?

4. What European nation took the first slaves? What other nations joined the slave trade?

5. Why did Europeans want colonies in Africa?

6. How did European imperialism change Africa?

One of the world's earliest civilizations was that of the ancient Egyptians, in northern Africa. The Egyptian pharaohs built great pyramids and temples. Many of these are still standing, thousands of years after they were built. In time, other nations founded colonies in northern Africa. The Phoenicians built the city of Carthage. Then the Romans came and built their own cities. Still later came the Arab conquerers. Their armies swept across northern Africa, bringing the Moslem religion with them.

But what about the rest of the continent of Africa? What about all the lands south of the big Sahara Desert?

Early Kingdoms

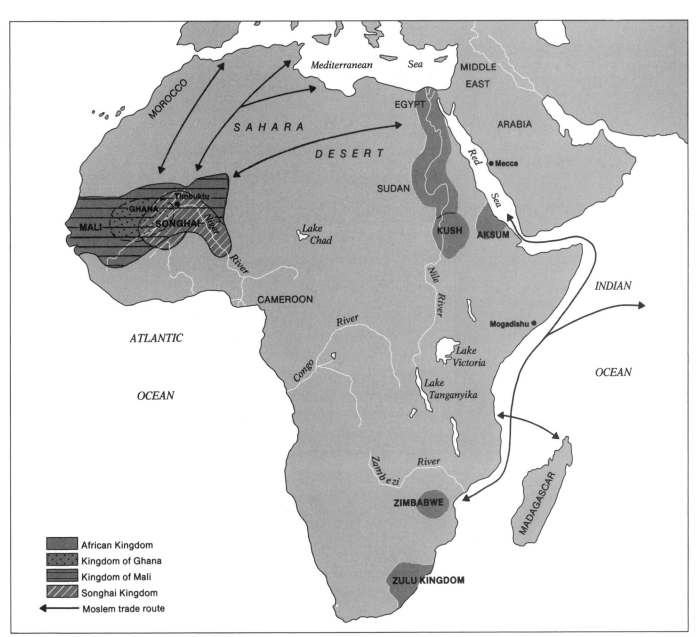

Ancient kingdoms of Africa

Along the Nile River, just south of Egypt, is a country called Sudan. During the time of ancient Egypt, this land was called Nubia. A civilization arose there about 2000 B.C. The people of Nubia, or Kush, as it was also called, were black. In about 1500 B.C., Egypt conquered Kush. For the next 500 years, Kush was ruled by the Egyptians. And the Kushites were greatly influenced by them. Kush became an important center of art, learning, and trade. But by about 1000 B.C., the Egyptians had lost much of their power. The Kushites were able to drive out the Egyptians.

At about this time, Kushites began mining iron. They used the iron to make tools and weapons. The Kushites kept growing stronger. In about 750 B.C., they conquered Egypt and ruled there until about 670 B.C.

The civilization of Kush lasted until about A.D. 350. Kush was then conquered by the neighboring kingdom of Aksum. By then both Kush and Aksum had come under the influence of the Roman Empire and Christianity. Nubia was to remain Christian until the 1300s when Arabs conquered the region. The Nubians then converted to the Moslem religion.

In western Africa, just on the southern edge of the Sahara Desert, is a vast area of grasslands. The land was populated by tribes of black Africans.

By about A.D. 1000, Arab traders from northern Africa began to cross the Sahara in **caravans.** The trade caravans brought goods that the people of western Africa needed. They brought tools and clothing. And they brought the thing that the people needed most—salt. The climate south of the Sahara is very hot and dry. People needed salt to stay healthy. They needed salt to preserve their food. Salt was so important that the people were willing to trade gold for it. Luckily there was plenty of gold available in western Africa.

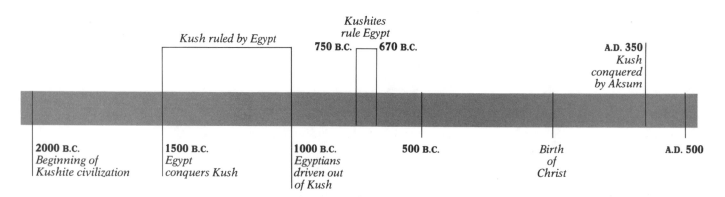

During the A.D. 300s, a kingdom called Ghana grew up in western Africa. The kingdom began to prosper about A.D. 1000. This is when the Arabs from northern Africa became interested in trade with Ghana. They had learned that Ghana was rich in gold. But trade turned out to be a mixed blessing. The Arab trading caravans brought not only goods but religion to Ghana, too. In time, Ghana's rulers became Moslems. But most of the people living in Ghana did not convert. They still practiced their own, ancient worship of many gods.

Moslem rulers tried to force the people to practice Islam. This weakened the kingdom. The Mandingo people of a kingdom called Mali took over Ghana near the end of the thirteenth century. By 1300 the kingdom of Ghana was gone, replaced by Mali.

The Kingdom of Ghana

From 1312 to 1337, the Mali kingdom was ruled by a man named Mansa Musa. *Mansa* means "king." Mansa Musa was a good king. He built Mali's wealth by encouraging and then taxing caravan trade. Mansa Musa was a Moslem. And he invited Arab scholars to come to Mali to teach. The city of Timbuktu became a center of Moslem learning.

Mansa Musa became famous when he made his pilgrimage to the holy city of Mecca, in Arabia. He decided to show the rest of the world just how wealthy his kingdom was. He took a splendid caravan with him on his pilgrimage to Mecca. Across the grasslands and deserts he went, along with thousands of his people. Mansa Musa took 500 slaves with him. Each slave carried a solid gold **staff**. He also took 100 camels, each loaded with bags of gold dust. Everywhere he went, the Mali ruler gave out gold and other gifts. Stories quickly spread about the fabulous wealth of the kingdom of Mali.

Mansa Musa, the Mali King

When Mansa Musa died, Mali weakened. A kingdom called Songhai took over control of Mali during the 1400s. One of the Songhai rulers was a king named Askia Mohammed. Askia ruled from 1493 to 1528. This was a time of growth in Songhai power. The city of Timbuktu reached its height as an important center of trade and of learning. Songhai remained strong until the late 1500s. Then the Moroccan king, Ahmed al-Mansur, The Victorious, attacked. The Moroccans had guns. The Songhai warriors fought with spears. Songhai was defeated.

The Kingdom of Songhai

Other Peoples of Africa

At about the time of Christ, a great migration began in Africa. Black peoples of what is now Nigeria and Cameroon moved southward into the forests of central Africa. The population had been growing, and the people needed more land. Migration continued for over the next 1,000 years. The people spoke Bantu languages. They settled in many parts of central, eastern, and southern Africa.

By about A.D. 1100, trading cities dotted the eastern African coast. A city called Mogadishu was one of the largest. The people living in coastal towns had frequent contact with Arab traders. They became Moslems, and they followed many Arabic customs. They spoke Swahili, a Bantu language that used many Arabic words. The language is still used in much of central and southern Africa.

Zulu warriors, 19th century

A number of kingdoms arose in southern Africa. One of these was the kingdom of Zimbabwe. Another was the kingdom of the Zulus. The Zulus had moved into southern Africa in the 1600s. They were powerful warriors. During the 1800s they had a strong military under a ruthless ruler named Shaka. Shaka led his armies to conquer other tribes. Meanwhile, southern Africa was being settled by the Dutch and the British. The Zulus fought against European rule. In 1879 the British defeated the Zulu kingdom.

The Europeans in Africa

Africa was not an easy land to explore. The Sahara Desert kept many European traders from traveling south by land. But during the Renaissance, interest in travel grew. Seamen sailed better ships. In the 1400s the Europeans began to arrive in Africa by sea routes.

The Portuguese were the first to sail the waters along Africa's coast. Prince Henry the Navigator sent ships along the west coast. He was searching for a trade route to India. Portuguese sailors soon learned of the gold in western Africa. They called a section of the African coastline the "Gold Coast."

In 1497 the Portuguese sea captain, Vasco da Gama, discovered the sea route around Africa. Soon Portugal set up trading posts along Africa's coasts. In 1571 Angola, in southwestern Africa, became a Portuguese colony.

Then the Portuguese found something in Africa that was a better money-maker than gold. They found that they could get rich by buying and selling human beings.

Slavery

There had been slaves in Africa for a long time. When tribes conquered other tribes, they often made slaves of their captives. But African slavery was very different from the kind of slavery the Europeans practiced. The Africans treated their slaves like human beings. Children of Africans' slaves were free. The Europeans treated their slaves like goods to be traded and sold, not like people.

The Portuguese were the first European slave traders. By the early 1500s, the Portuguese were capturing Africans and packing them onto crowded ships. Many Africans died on the terrible voyages. Those who survived had to work as slaves in mines and on plantations in the West Indies. Soon the Spanish were also shipping slaves to the Americas.

The lower deck of a slave ship

By the mid-1600s, the French, English, and Dutch had joined in the profitable slave trade. Some Africans helped supply the Europeans with slaves. Tribes fought each other to capture people to supply the slave traders. The fighting between tribes weakened Africa.

The slave markets wanted only the healthiest, strongest young Africans. Over time about 10 million men and women were taken out of Africa to be sold as slaves. The loss of some of its finest people also weakened Africa. Africa was in no position to defend itself against European imperialism.

The End of Slavery

Fortunately, people finally recognized that slavery was wrong. By the 1800s many countries made slave trading illegal. In 1834 Britain outlawed slavery in its colonies. Other European countries soon did the same. The United States abolished slavery in 1865. By 1888 slavery was illegal throughout the Americas.

European Imperialism

The slave trade finally came to an end. But Africa had not seen the end of European **dominance** and European **prejudice**. In the 1800s there had been an industrial revolution in Europe. Now Europeans needed raw materials and new markets for finished products. European nations wanted new colonies. And the continent of Africa had lots of land.

The Industrial Revolution led to imperialism. But there was also another reason that led the Europeans into Africa. That was **racism**. Some Europeans simply thought they were better than the dark-skinned peoples of the world. Some thought it was their "duty" to bring their own culture to the black Africans. So the Europeans took over Africa. European explorers moved away from the coastline and into the very heart of the continent.

Europe Divides Up Africa

In 1884 European nations held a **conference** in Berlin, Germany. The United States and Turkey sent representatives, too. No one invited African representatives. The conference set up rules for forming colonies in Africa. When the conference ended, one of the greatest land grabs in history began. By 1914 Europeans had taken over almost all the land in Africa.

The Europeans formed some of their colonies very easily. They made agreements with local tribal chiefs. They gave the chiefs presents and promised chances for trade. Some of the tribal leaders simply gave away their kingdoms.

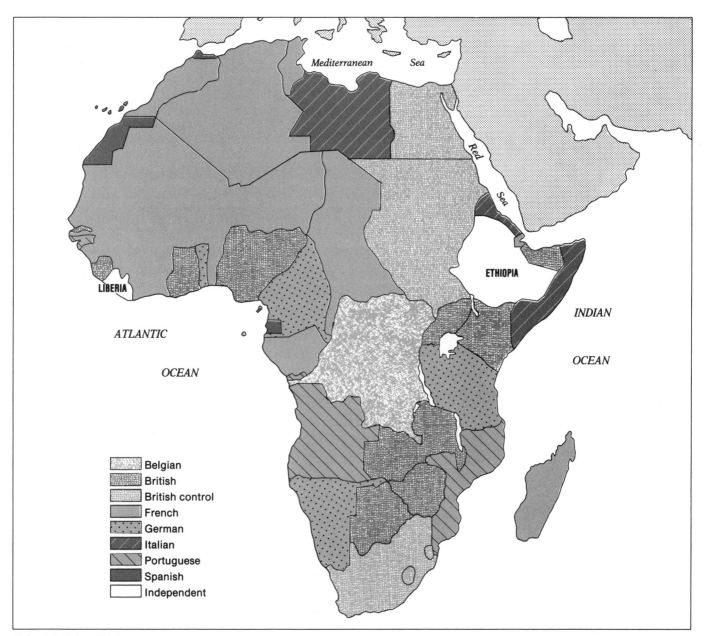

Legend:
- Belgian
- British
- British control
- French
- German
- Italian
- Portuguese
- Spanish
- Independent

Colonial Africa, 1914

European missionaries helped set up colonies. They had come to convert the Africans to Christianity. Often they were very unwelcome. But again, the Europeans felt it was their duty to show Africans a "better way."

Soon there were only two independent countries left in all of Africa. Ethiopia, in the northeast, was the larger one. The little country of Liberia, on the west coast, was the other. It had been founded in 1822 by blacks from the United States. It had declared its independence in 1847.

Life in Colonial Africa

It is easy to see the wrongs and injustices of European imperialism in Africa. African culture was damaged. The Europeans did not understand tribal differences and tribal customs. They did not even try to understand.

The Europeans forced the Africans to learn new ways. They tried to make the Africans feel **inferior**. They forced the Africans to accept European government, religion, and languages. They drew up colonial boundaries without giving any thought to splitting up tribes.

Some of the things the Europeans did in Africa helped the natives. But most of those things were done for the sake of the Europeans. Railway systems, roads, and schools were built. And the continent of Africa was opened up to the rest of the world.

In the years ahead, new ideas would come to Africa. These would be ideas of freedom, of self-government, and, in some cases, of revolution.

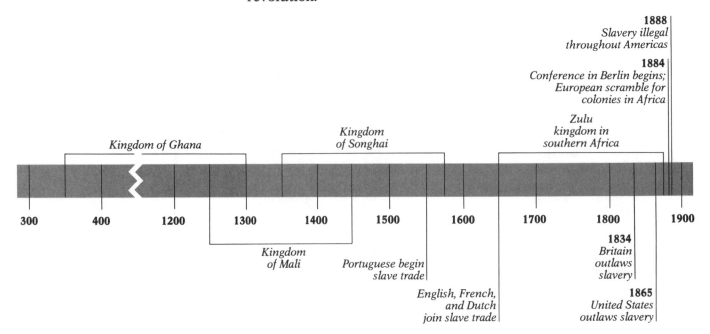

Kingdom of Ghana

Kingdom of Mali

Kingdom of Songhai

Portuguese begin slave trade

English, French, and Dutch join slave trade

Zulu kingdom in southern Africa

1834
Britain outlaws slavery

1865
United States outlaws slavery

1884
Conference in Berlin begins; European scramble for colonies in Africa

1888
Slavery illegal throughout Americas

300   400   1200   1300   1400   1500   1600   1700   1800   1900

Points to Remember

♦ The ancient African civilization of Kush was greatly influenced by the Egyptians.

♦ There were rich kingdoms called Ghana, Mali, and Songhai in western Africa.

♦ Europeans began arriving in Africa by sea in the 1400s.

♦ The Portuguese found that they could make money by taking Africans abroad and selling them as slaves.

♦ The British, French, and Dutch soon joined the slave trade.

♦ The Industrial Revolution and racial prejudices played a part in European colonization of Africa.

♦ In 1884 a conference in Berlin laid down ground rules for colonizing Africa.

♦ By 1914 almost the entire continent of Africa had fallen under European imperialism.

Think About It!

1. Who was Mansa Musa? How did a pilgrimage to Mecca make him famous?

2. What were the differences between early African slavery and the European slave trade?

3. Why were Europeans able to set up African colonies so easily in the nineteenth century?

4. Give examples showing that Europeans practiced racism in the African colonies.

Chapter 10

Back to Europe: The Unification of Italy and of Germany

Words to Know

anthem   the official song of a country

chancellor   the head of government, or prime minister, in some European countries

confederation   a group of independent states joined together for a purpose

diplomat   a person in government whose job is dealing with other countries

legislature   a group of persons who make the laws of a nation or state

militarism   a national policy of maintaining a powerful army and constant readiness for war

nationalism   strong loyalty to one's culture and nation

prime minister   the chief official of the government in some countries

societies   groups of people joined together for a common purpose

unification   bringing together into one whole

volunteers   those who offer to do something of their own free will

Look for the answers as you read:

1. What is nationalism? Where does nationalism develop?

2. How did the spirit of nationalism lead to the unification of Italy?

3. Who were three men who helped unify Italy?

4. How did Napoleon's actions help the spirit of nationalism to develop in Germany?

5. Why was Prussia the strongest state in Germany?

6. How did Prime Minister Otto von Bismarck unite Germany under a Prussian kaiser?

7. How did Bismarck's "blood and iron" policy set the tone for future Germans?

Nationalism is a feeling of strong loyalty to one's country and culture. Such a feeling often develops among people who speak the same language and follow similar customs. Nationalism leads people to honor their flag and to sing a national **anthem**. It leads people to risk their very lives to support their nation.

The spirit of nationalism helped the French fight off countries that were against their revolution. It gave the colonies in the Americas the strength to break away from the European imperialists.

In the nineteenth century, the spirit of nationalism led to the **unification** of Italy and Germany. In both places people were feeling the bonds of language and customs and culture. They decided it was time to unite as single nations.

Italy before unification

Nationalism in Italy

During the early Roman times, Italy had been a united country. It was the center of the Roman Empire. But late in the A.D. 400s, the Roman Empire fell. Italy was divided into many small kingdoms. For more than a thousand years, different nations and monarchs fought for control of the Italian territories. French troops, Spanish troops, German troops; all marched through Italy. Then in 1796, Napoleon Bonaparte invaded the Italian peninsula and took power.

Napoleon granted Venetia to Austria. Venetia was the kingdom that included the city of Venice. Napoleon put the rest of the small kingdoms under his own rule. In 1804 he crowned himself ruler of the new kingdom. The crown he wore bore these words: "God gave it [the Italian peninsula] to me; woe to him who dares touch it."

Napoleon's actions gave rise to the spirit of nationalism. This spirit would one day carry Italy to independence. Napoleon did away with old boundary lines and joined the little kingdoms together. By doing this, he gave Italians a chance to look at themselves as members of one group. The idea that all of them were Italians began to grow.

Napoleon invading Italy

As feelings of nationalism grew, Italians began to think about unity. They dreamed about one independent Italy. But by 1815, Italy was once again divided into many kingdoms and states. Most of these were either ruled by Austria or by the pope. Those who wanted to unify Italy had some barriers to overcome.

Austria tried to crush any ideas of unity. Austria wanted Italy to remain weak and divided. The pope also tried to crush any ideas of unity. He feared nationalism as a threat to his own power.

But the people wanted to be free. They wanted to join together as one nation. So secret revolutionary **societies** sprang up. During the mid-1800s, three men became leaders of the movement toward a unified Italy. Italians called these men "The Soul," "The Brain," and "The Sword."

Secret Societies

The Soul of Italy was a man named Giuseppe Mazzini. In 1830 he joined a group that was working to unify Italy. That same year he was exiled because of his political activities. He would remain in exile for 18 years. In 1832 Mazzini organized a secret society known as "Young Italy." The society's goal was to free the Italian peninsula from Austrian rule. Young Italy wanted to join the country together under one government.

In 1848 revolutions broke out in many European countries. Mazzini returned to Italy to stir up a revolution there. The ruler of the kingdom of Sardinia favored the revolutionaries. He tried to help their cause by declaring war on Austria. But Austrian and French armies helped put down the Italian revolt. Not only did the revolution fail, but Sardinia was also defeated. Mazzini had to go into exile once again.

The Austrians forced the Sardinian king from his throne. His son, Victor Emmanuel II, became king of Sardinia in 1849.

"The Soul"

Giuseppe Mazzini

The new king of Sardinia was also in favor of Italian unity. He named Camillo di Cavour as his **prime minister**. This act moved Italy closer to freedom. Camillo di Cavour would soon be known as "The Brain," the clever leader of the unification movement.

"The Brain"

Cavour was a **diplomat**, a master of foreign affairs. He recognized Austria as an enemy to unification. In 1858 he arranged a defense agreement between Sardinia and France. The next year Austria declared war on Sardinia. But French and Italian soldiers pushed the Austrians almost as far east as Venice. Sardinia gained the nearby region of Lombardy. Then in 1860, people from Modena, Parma, and Tuscany showed their respect for Sardinia's accomplishments. They united with Sardinia and turned against Austria.

Count Camillo di Cavour

"The Sword"

Giuseppe Garibaldi

Giuseppe Garibaldi was a revolutionary most of his life. When he was 26, he joined the secret society, Young Italy. Garibaldi was a soldier in the battle for freedom. His attempts to lead Italy to independence won him the nickname of "The Sword."

Failed rebellions forced Garibaldi to flee Italy or face death. He returned in 1848 to fight under Mazzini. When this revolution failed, he went into exile again.

In 1859 Garibaldi was back in Italy. He joined the fight for freedom led by King Victor Emmanuel of Sardinia. Garibaldi led an army of 1,000 **volunteers** to Sicily. His men were called "Red Shirts" because they wore red wool shirts as uniforms.

When Garibaldi and his army reached Sicily, many Sicilians joined them. Sicily was soon free. Then Garibaldi, The Sword, led his army north on the Italian mainland. He headed for Naples. Cavour, The Brain, sent an army south. By the end of 1860, the two armies had freed most of Italy. In 1861 Victor Emmanuel II became ruler of an almost completely united Italy.

Unification, at Last

Only Rome and the northern kingdom of Venetia were still under foreign control. The pope ruled Rome and Austria ruled Venetia. In 1866 the Italians helped Prussia defeat Austria in war. In return for its support, Italy was given Venetia.

Italy after unification

Then came Rome. Garibaldi tried to take Rome twice, but failed. He was defeated by French troops who came to aid the pope. In 1870 Italy got another chance at Rome. France was fighting a war against Prussia. France took its troops out of Rome to help fight the Prussians. It was Italy's time to move! The pope's own small army could not fight off the Italian troops. Rome finally became part of the united nation of Italy. And in 1871, Rome became the capital of Italy.

Nationalism in Germany

Just as he did in Italy, Napoleon lit the first flames of nationalism in Germany. Napoleon took over large parts of Germany in 1806. These lands were made up of many small kingdoms. Napoleon decided to join them together to rule them more easily. He called the group of kingdoms the **confederation** of the Rhine. People living within the confederation began to have a sense of loyalty toward one another.

Germany before unification

When Napoleon was defeated in 1815, a new German confederation was formed. Thirty-nine states, including Austria and Prussia, were joined together. Since Austria was large, it considered itself the leader. But Prussia had a well-organized government and real strength—military strength.

Many Germans thought about unifying the states under a central government. But Austria was against German unity. Austrians thought they could remain more powerful with the German states divided. It was not until 1862 that Germany moved toward becoming one nation.

Otto von Bismarck

The king of Prussia, Wilhelm I, was having problems with his **legislature**. King Wilhelm wanted to add to his already mighty army. But the legislature would not give him the money that he needed. So King Wilhelm turned to a Prussian landowner and soldier to help him. In 1862 he appointed a new prime minister, Otto von Bismarck.

Otto von Bismarck had a strong sense of Prussian loyalty. Bismarck was not interested in democracy or individual rights. He believed that duty to one's country was most important.

Bismarck promised the Prussian king a firm hand over the legislature and the people. The new prime minister thought that could be accomplished with a strong army. "The importance of a state," Bismarck said, "is measured by the number of soldiers it can put into the field of battle. . . ."

Bismarck followed a policy of "blood and iron." In other words, it was a policy of war. "The great questions of our day," he said, "cannot be settled by speeches and majority votes, but by blood and iron."

Bismarck encouraged King Wilhelm to unite the German states under one rule—Prussian rule.

How was this to be done? Bismarck's answer was war!

Otto von Bismarck

The Unification of Germany

In 1864 Bismarck began a war with Denmark. After just seven months of fighting, Prussia seized two provinces from Denmark.

In 1866 Bismarck set out after his main goal—Austria. Seven weeks later, Austria gave in to Bismarck.

Then Prussia formed the North German Confederation in 1867. Most of the German states joined. The Confederation's seat of power was Prussia. And at its head was Wilhelm I.

Bismarck would not be satisfied until all the German states were united under Wilhelm's rule. He decided on the best way to join the states. He would rally them together against one common enemy. For that purpose, in 1870, Bismarck started a war with France. Prussia's mighty armies won easily. They took the provinces of Alsace and Lorraine as their prize.

Germany after unification

Kaiser Wilhelm I

At the end of the war, all German states joined with Prussia. They formed a united German empire. On January 18, 1871, the new German Empire was officially declared. It was also called the "Second Reich." King Wilhelm I of Prussia was crowned its emperor, or "kaiser." This title came from the Latin word *Caesar*.

The German Nation

There were two main features of the new Germany. Each would have tremendous effects on the world in the years ahead.

First, Germany was not a democratic nation. Germans accepted rule by a single person. Bismarck became the **chancellor** of Germany.

He was responsible only to Kaiser Wilhelm I. Neither the kaiser nor the chancellor had to answer to any legislature nor to any elected representatives. These two men alone had complete power in Germany.

Second, Germany had a strong tradition of **militarism**. Bismarck's "blood and iron" policy had become the German way. German nationalism meant pride in a mighty military force.

Germans gave their soldiers respect and honor. It was a German man's privilege to belong to a great army. It was an honor to fight for the glory of the empire.

All of Germany was geared toward a strong military. Large businesses supported the army. Industrialists, like Friedrich Krupp of the Krupp Iron and Steel Works, devoted factories to making war machines. Krupp built guns and cannons. The whole nation stood behind the military effort. Germany was ready for war!

Krupp armament factory, Essen, Germany

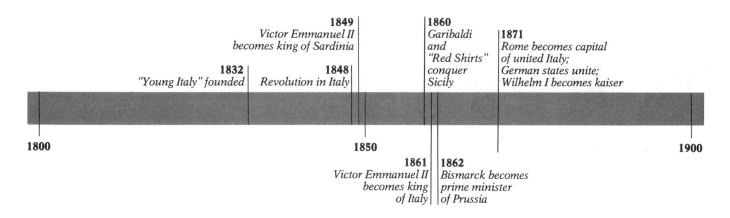

Points to Remember

◆ The spirit of nationalism led the people of Italy to unite under a central government.

◆ During the nineteenth century, the Italians worked toward independence and unification.

◆ In 1870 Italy was totally united.

◆ Sardinia's King Victor Emmanuel II became the King of Italy.

◆ During the nineteenth century many Germans wanted to see a unified Germany.

◆ Austria opposed the unification of Germany.

◆ The Prime Minister of Prussia, Otto von Bismarck, waged many wars in a movement toward unification.

◆ Bismarck won his wars, and in 1871 Germany was united.

◆ Prussia's Wilhelm I became the kaiser of the German Empire.

◆ Germany was not a democracy.

◆ Germany had a strong tradition of militarism.

Think About It!

1. Why was Giuseppe Garibaldi called the Sword of Italy?

2. Who ruled the newly unified Italy? Who ruled the newly unified Germany?

3. What does the phrase "blood and iron" mean?

4. How did industrialists contribute to German militarism?

5. What would Germany's militarism mean to the world?

Chapter 11

World War I

Words to Know

alliances nations joined together for some purpose

armistice an agreement to stop fighting, a truce before a formal peace treaty

casualties soldiers who have been killed, wounded, captured, or are missing

fronts the different places where the actual fighting is going on during a war

neutral joining neither side in a war

sniper a person who shoots from a hidden spot

submarines warships that travel under the water

torpedoed attacked with a large, exploding, cigar-shaped missile

trenches long ditches dug in the ground to protect soldiers in battle

Look for the answers as you read:

1. What is meant by a "balance of power"?

2. What were the two alliances made in 1914?

3. What event directly caused World War I?

4. When did the United States enter the war?

5. How did the presence of U.S. soldiers and supplies affect the outcome of the war?

6. What were the terms of peace at the end of the war?

World War I began on July 28, 1914. No one nation wanted a war. But in truth, all the major powers in Europe had been gathering military strength for many years.

The nationalism of the 1800s led to stronger armies. People who were loyal to their own nations felt that military strength showed pride and power.

The imperialism of the 1800s also created a need for strong armies. Nations had their colonies to protect. Each nation feared that it might lose what it had without a strong military.

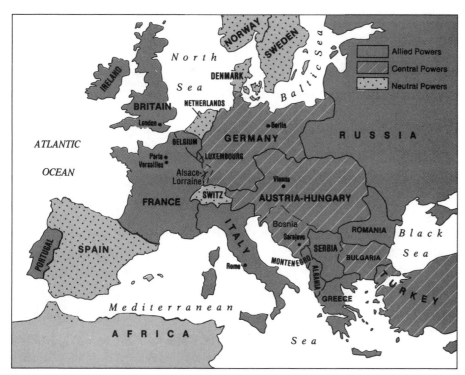

Europe, 1914

The Balance of Power

Relations between countries were strained in the early 1900s. By 1914 Europe had divided itself into two sides. Nations formed **alliances**. They promised to protect each other and to help each other in case of war.

One group of nations was called the Central Powers. The nations of the Central Powers included Germany, Austria-Hungary, the Ottoman Empire (Turkey), and, for a short time, Italy. The other group of nations was called the Allies. On that side were Britain, France, and Russia.

Each alliance tried to keep the other from getting too strong. They wanted to keep a "balance of power" in Europe.

Rising Tensions

As the year 1914 began, there was tension throughout Europe. France and Germany had been bitter enemies for years. France had lost a war against Bismarck's armies in 1871. Ever since then, France wanted to get back the provinces of Alsace and Lorraine.

Russia faced an ongoing quarrel with Austria-Hungary. They disagreed about the territorial borders in the Balkans.

Nations watched each other as each built up its military forces. Airplanes, bigger warships, and machine guns made armies more capable of destruction. One country would build new arms. Then another would panic and race to keep up. No one wanted war, but everyone was getting ready.

The War Begins

It took a single incident in July of 1914 to explode the already tense situation in Europe. The Austrian Archduke Francis Ferdinand was assassinated. This is named as the incident that began the First World War.

Archduke Ferdinand was the next in line to the throne of Austria-Hungary. He and his wife, Sophie, were visiting Sarajevo, a city in the Austrian province of Bosnia. Many Serbs also lived in Bosnia. And some of them believed Bosnia should belong to Serbia.

Archduke Ferdinand and his wife were traveling by motor car on a road in Sarajevo. They were a fine-looking pair. The Archduke wore a white uniform, and his wife wore a matching white gown. Riding in an open car, they were clear targets. As the royal procession drove through the streets, two shots rang out. Archduke Ferdinand and his wife were both killed by a **sniper**.

The assassin, Gavrilo Princip, was a Serb. He was a member of a Serbian revolutionary group called the "Black Hand."

Austria-Hungary blamed the Serbian government for the assassination. On July 28, 1914, it declared war on Serbia. Now the alliances came into play. Germany stood behind Austria-Hungary. Russia came to the aid of Serbia. France came to Russia's aid. Soon England joined in to help its allies. World War I had begun.

The assassination of Archduke Francis Ferdinand

The Great War

World War I is sometimes called "The Great War." It was not really a "worldwide" war. Most of the fighting took place in Europe. And not every country in the world was fighting. However, more than 30 countries, including all the major powers, were involved. The Great War's effects were certainly felt worldwide.

At first the Central Powers seemed to be winning. Germany and Austria-Hungary, joined by Turkey and Bulgaria, made gains. Italy had been allied with the Central Powers. But it remained **neutral** in the early part of the war. Then in 1915, Italy changed its alliance. It joined forces with the Allies.

Trench Warfare

The Central Powers wanted to take France. They came within 25 miles of Paris. But the French and British held them off in a major battle, the Battle of the Marne. Then both sides dug in. The soldiers dug long **trenches**. Armies could hide in the trenches and shoot at each other.

The **fronts** were lined with networks of trenches. There were three fronts in Europe. The Western Front ran from Belgium to Switzerland. The Eastern Front ran from the Baltic Sea to the Black Sea. The Italian, or Southern, Front ran between Italy and Austria-Hungary.

The battle trenches along the fronts became home for the soldiers. They ate in the trenches and slept in the trenches. And many soldiers died in the trenches.

Most of the battles of World War I were fought inside Europe. But there was also some fighting in Africa and in the Middle East. The powerful British navy kept control of most of the seas.

Warfare in the trenches

The United States Enters the War

Despite Britain's great navy, German **submarines** were terrorizing the oceans. They attacked enemy merchant ships without warning. Then in 1915, a British luxury liner, the *Lusitania*, was **torpedoed** and sunk. The death list of 1,198 persons included 128 Americans. In 1917 the submarines began attacking ships of neutral nations. Several American merchant ships were sunk.

The sinking of the Lusitania

In April 1917, U.S. president Woodrow Wilson made an announcement. He said that it was time to "make the world safe for democracy." The United States declared war on Germany and joined the Allies. The United States entered the battlefields at a good time. The Allies needed help. The United States sent fresh soldiers and supplies of arms to Europe. The scale in the balance of power was now tipped in favor of the Allies.

Then in November of 1917, a revolution took place in Russia. The new government signed a peace treaty with Germany and pulled out of the war.

The End of the War

With new American soldiers and supplies, the Allies began to push back the Germans. The other Central Powers had given up. Germany stood alone, and German armies were losing ground.

Germany asked for an end to the war. On November 11, 1918, an **armistice** was declared. All fighting was to stop at 11:00 A.M. that day.

After the war, leaders of the Allied nations and Germany met in Versailles, France. Their purpose was to write a peace treaty. The treaty, which was signed in 1919, made many demands on Germany.

Germany lost all of its colonies and had to return Alsace and Lorraine to France. Germany took all blame for the war, so it had to pay for many of the war's costs. And Germany promised to disarm. The nation was not supposed to rebuild its navy or air force. And it could maintain only a small army. This was quite a blow to a nation that had taken such pride in a powerful military.

Another big loser in the war was Turkey. In 1900 most of the Middle East and North Africa was still ruled by the Ottoman Turks. But the end of the war brought about the end of the Ottoman Empire. Most of the Arab lands that had been ruled by the Turks now fell under British control.

The Treaty of Versailles

Europe after World War I

Results of the War

The Great War ended four years after it had begun. Those four years meant the loss of almost eight million soldiers. Millions of others died, too. They died of disease and of starvation, side effects of war. Russia suffered the most **casualties** in World War I.

The total cost of the war to all countries involved was more than $337,000,000,000. All of Europe was weakened.

Wartime Inventions

The war brought many changes to the world. New inventions were perfected in a hurry to meet war needs. The Germans developed submarines to travel under the water like sharks. The submarines were also called "U-boats" (underwater boats). They moved unseen, seeking their prey.

Allied countries could not find a defense against the submarines for the first three years of the war. Eventually depth charges were used to destroy the submarines. Fast British ships known as "subchasers" carried the depth charges. These ships also used zigzag courses to avoid German submarines.

The submarines were very successful. Only 203 German submarines were destroyed during the whole war. But the German submarines sank 6,604 Allied ships.

For the first time, airplanes were used for war. At first they were just used for scouting, watching the enemy, and taking pictures. They were not used for fighting until later in the war.

Planes were improved rapidly. In 1914 an airplane could go 90 miles an hour. By 1917 they were flying at 175 miles an hour. They carried bombs and machine guns. Some pilots became famous as "war aces" for shooting down five or more enemy airplanes.

Germany used "zeppelins" in the air. Zeppelins were huge, cigar-shaped crafts, 600 feet long. They were inflated with hydrogen gas and used in bombing raids over England and France.

British engineers invented the tank, an armored vehicle with caterpillar tracks. The big tanks rumbled their way across the battlefields of Europe. And there were other new weapons, like poison gas and flame throwers. Each side tried to outdo the other with more powerful and more horrible weaponry.

Allied fighter planes: Sopwith F-1 "Camel"

The League of Nations: A Peacekeeper

When the war ended, leaders of the world's nations looked at the results. Millions were dead. The costs were tremendous. Countries were left weakened. They decided there must be a better way to solve conflicts between nations.

So in 1920, the League of Nations was set up. Its headquarters were in Geneva, Switzerland—a neutral, peaceful country. Representatives of member nations could meet there to discuss their problems. It was the first organization designed to keep the peace of the entire world.

Many nations, including the United States, did not join the league. Americans decided that they did not want to get involved in Europe's problems again. The league had no army to enforce its decisions. It was based on good will and the idea that nations wanted peace. The war years, 1914 to 1918, had left everyone fearful of war. Now the whole world was anxious to avoid war. And it was hopeful that a war would never be fought again.

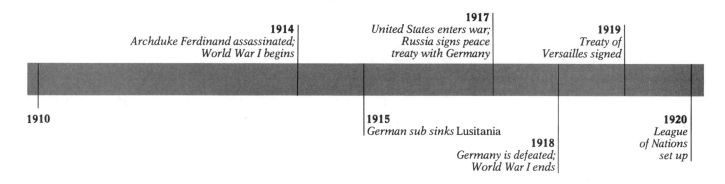

1914 — Archduke Ferdinand assassinated; World War I begins

1917 — United States enters war; Russia signs peace treaty with Germany

1919 — Treaty of Versailles signed

1910

1915 — German sub sinks Lusitania

1918 — Germany is defeated; World War I ends

1920 — League of Nations set up

Points to Remember

◆ World War I began in July 1914. An armistice was declared in November 1918.

◆ Before the war, tensions were building between two European alliances. One alliance, the Central Powers, included Germany and Austria-Hungary, and, for a time, Italy. The Allies included Britain, France, and Russia. When the war began, Italy was neutral. But in 1915 it joined the Allies.

◆ The two alliances hoped to keep a balance of power in Europe.

◆ The assassination of Austrian Archduke Francis Ferdinand triggered World War I.

◆ The United States joined the war on the side of the Allies in 1917.

◆ Russia withdrew from the war, signing a peace treaty with Germany in 1917.

◆ American forces and supplies helped the Allies win the war.

◆ The Treaty of Versailles, signed in 1919, set up terms for peace.

◆ Wartime developments included the submarine, improved airplanes, and more powerful weaponry.

◆ The League of Nations was set up after the war in the hope of maintaining world peace.

Think About It!

1. Explain how each of the following led to World War I:
   (a) militarism
   (b) nationalism
   (c) imperialism

2. If not every country was involved in World War I, why was it called a "World War"?

3. When the war ended in 1918, what were the final costs in lives and in dollars? Which country suffered the most casualties?

4. What military inventions came out of World War I?

Chapter 12

The Changing World: The Soviet Union

Words to Know

censor to examine communications before they are released and to remove any parts that are objected to

collective run by a group; a *collective* farm

communism a political system based on an absence of social class, common ownership of industries and farms, and a sharing of work and of goods produced

councils groups of people who meet to plan something, give advice, and make laws and rules

dialects forms of a language used only in a certain place or among a certain group

geography the natural surface features of the earth, or any part of it

Look for the answers as you read:

1. Who was Ivan the Terrible, and why was he so "terrible"?

2. What did Peter the Great mean by opening a "window to the West"?

3. How did "Bloody Sunday" touch off the Revolution of 1905?

4. How did the common people of Russia feel about Russia's involvement in World War I?

5. Who was Karl Marx and what did he believe?

6. Who were the Bolsheviks, and who was Vladimir Ilyich Lenin?

7. What kind of leader was Joseph Stalin?

The Soviet Union

The **geography** of the Soviet Union is varied. The country takes in frozen wastelands, thick forests, and wide plains known as "steppes." There are also sandy deserts and huge snow-capped mountains. And some of the longest rivers in the world are in the Soviet Union.

The people of the Soviet Union are just as varied as the geography. Some are tall and blond haired, others are olive skinned and dark haired. Altogether, Soviet peoples speak more than 200 different languages and **dialects.**

The Soviet Union is the largest country on earth. But the country was not always so large, and it was not always strong. Russia did not become the powerful Soviet Union until after World War I.

In A.D. 1237 a Mongol leader named Batu Khan invaded Russia with a huge army. Batu was a grandson of Genghis Khan. He destroyed one town after another. Russia became part of the Mongol empire.

The Early History of Russia

The Mongols ruled for over 200 years. Then they grew weaker because of fighting among their leaders. Finally, in 1480 a group of Russian princes defeated the Mongols. Ivan III and his son, Basil III, led those princes. In 1547 Basil's son became the ruler, the first czar of all Russia. The word "czar" comes from the Latin word *Caesar*. The first czar's name was Ivan IV. He became known as Ivan the Terrible.

Why Was Ivan So "Terrible"?

Ivan the Terrible

Ivan IV changed Russian government. Earlier rulers, called Grand Dukes, had accepted advice and criticism from other nobles. Not Ivan IV. As czar he moved the head of the government to Moscow and made himself all-powerful. It is said that one nobleman who dared to disagree with Ivan IV was tossed to the hounds. And he was torn to shreds!

Ivan ruled by terror. With threats of cruel punishment, he frightened the Russian people into doing his bidding. Hundreds of people were murdered by Ivan and his special police force. Ivan even killed his oldest son with his own two hands.

Ivan fought many wars. He increased Russia's territory. But he worsened the daily lives of his people. Under Ivan the Terrible, the peasants were dreadfully poor. There was lots of land. But there were not enough people to keep the economy strong.

Ivan did grant the right to trade in Russia. This brought in money for the upper classes. But it did little to improve the lives of the common people. After Ivan, most Russian rulers would seem kindly in comparison.

Contact with Europe

The coronation of Czar Michael Romanov, 1613

During the 1600s, Russia added to its territory. It took over the Ukraine. And it extended its control of Siberia eastward to the Pacific Ocean. Slowly Russia increased its contact with the rest of the world. Czar Michael Romanov took the throne in 1613. He encouraged trade with Holland and England. And he brought foreign engineers and doctors to Russia. Michael's son Alexis followed him. He, too, was open to European customs and cultures.

Peter the Great

Toward the end of the seventeenth century, a czar named Peter ruled in Russia. Peter had big plans. He wanted to make Russia more powerful. His goal was to make Russia equal to the nations of western Europe. So Peter brought more Europeans into Russia. He brought engineers, artists, soldiers, and scientists to teach Russians the ways of Western Europe.

Still, Peter did not learn all he wanted to know. So he went on a journey. He traveled to the Netherlands to study shipbuilding. And he continued his studies in England, where he visited factories, schools, and museums. He also visited France, Germany, and Austria.

When Czar Peter returned, he had many new ideas. He wanted to "westernize" his people. He ordered his subjects to wear European-style clothing instead of long, Oriental-type robes. He demanded that all Russian men cut off their beards to look more European. To set an example, Peter called his nobles together and cut off their beards himself. When people rebelled against Peter's no-beard orders, he demanded a tax from any man wearing a beard.

Peter the Great

Peter changed the old Russian calendar to make it match the European calendar. He gave women more freedom. He put the Russian church under complete control of his government.

Peter's desire to "westernize" Russia led him to his quest for a "window to the West." Peter wanted to open a Russian port on the ice-free Baltic Sea. But Sweden stood in his way, so in 1700 he attacked Sweden. The war lasted until 1721. A peace treaty gave Russia land along the eastern Baltic coast.

Meanwhile, in 1703 Peter began building the city of St. Petersburg. This would be his European "window." It was built along the Neva River, where the river flows into the Gulf of Finland. In 1712 Peter moved the nation's capital from Moscow to St. Petersburg. Today St. Petersburg is called Leningrad.

Peter brought new ideas, industrialization, and strength to Russia. That is why he was given the title "Peter the Great." But he did little for common people. Russian peasants were still poor and completely at the mercy of their czar.

Smolny Convent, St. Petersburg

Fontanka Canal, St. Petersburg

Catherine the Great

In 1762 Empress Catherine II ruled Russia. Catherine continued many of Peter's policies. She kept the "window to the West" open. She brought French culture to the nobles of Russia and improved their education.

But Catherine, too, did little for the peasants. In 1773 Catherine's armies had to put down a peasant revolt.

Napoleon in Russia

France's Napoleon Bonaparte invaded Russia in 1812. It turned out to be Napoleon's biggest mistake. The Russian armies fled from the French. Napoleon reached Moscow and easily took the city. But then Russians burned their own city down. When the weather turned bitter cold, Napoleon ordered a retreat from Russia. On the long march home, the men suffered from hunger and freezing temperatures. And there were constant attacks from the Russian army. Less than half of Napoleon's men lived to reach France. The great Russian author Tolstoy wrote about Napoleon's invasion of Russia in his famous novel, *War and Peace*.

"Bloody Sunday" and the 1905 Revolution

Russian peasants had lived under a feudal-type system for hundreds of years. Wealthy nobles owned all the farmlands. As industrialization came to Russia, factories sprang up in the cities. Thousands of peasants left the farms. They moved to the cities to work in those factories. Often the peasants found the factory owners as unfair and uncaring as the land-owning nobles had been.

On a cold Sunday, January 22, 1905, a large group of men, women, and children gathered in St. Petersburg. They were the city's factory workers. Over 200,000 came together to protest working conditions. Their leader, a priest named Father Gapon, carried a letter for Czar Nicholas II. The letter asked for better working conditions. And it also asked for representation of the common people in the legislature.

The workers gathered peacefully. They marched to the czar's Winter Palace, singing "God Save the Czar." They did not realize that Nicholas II had already left the palace. They did not know they would be met by an army of the czar's soldiers.

Street fighting during the 1905 revolution

The soldiers were under no specific orders. They panicked when they saw the mob approaching the palace. They opened fire on the marchers. Hundreds of men, women, and children were shot and killed or wounded that day. January 22, 1905, became known as Russia's "Bloody Sunday."

Bloody Sunday was the end of any peaceful demand for change. Strikes, riots, and revolutionary battles broke out. In order to put a stop to the revolt, Nicholas II agreed to set up an elected *Duma*, or parliament. The Duma would have the power to rule on any proposals for new laws. Some people were satisfied with this change. Others felt that the Duma was not enough. But the Dumas lasted until 1917.

The Revolutionaries and Karl Marx

Many of the revolutionaries in Russia had read the works of Karl Marx. Marx was a German thinker of the 1800s. He had explained his ideas in the *Communist Manifesto*, which was published in 1848. He believed it was wrong for factory owners to make most of the money. He said the workers should share in the profits of their work. He encouraged workers to rise up against the middle class. Marx pictured a perfect world where there would be no classes and where government would be unnecessary. Marx's ideas were known as **communism**. Some of the revolutionaries in Russia wanted to see Marx's ideas become a reality in their country.

Karl Marx

Russia entered World War I shortly after it began in 1914. The war brought severe food shortages to Russia. The poor people became even poorer. The common people of Russia were not interested in fighting Germany. But Czar Nicholas II had plunged Russia into the war.

In March 1917 the people of Russia demanded more food. The starving workers and peasants revolted. Czar Nicholas II was overthrown, and a new government took over. The government promised democracy in Russia. It did not, however, end Russia's involvement in World War I. The people were against the war. It was draining supplies, killing the men, and taking the food.

World War I and the Overthrow of Czar Nicholas II

Later that year, a man named Vladimir Ilyich Lenin returned to Russia from exile in Switzerland. Lenin had always hated the government of the czar. His brother had been hanged as a revolutionary. And Lenin himself had been exiled.

Lenin read Karl Marx. He became a communist revolutionary who believed in rebellion and in a classless society. On his return to Russia, Lenin became the leader of a communist group called the Bolsheviks. "Bolshevik" means "member of the majority." Lenin and the Bolsheviks promised to give the people what they wanted: "Peace, land, and bread."

In November 1917 the Bolsheviks overthrew the government. Karl Marx had pictured a society with no need for government. But Lenin felt that a strict Communist party should be in charge. The country would need a planned economy. And the Communist party would draw up the plans. The country would be governed by **councils** called "soviets." The soviets would be headed by Bolsheviks.

Lenin and the Bolshevik Revolution

In 1918 Moscow became the nation's capital once again. That year Russia was torn apart by a civil war. The Communists had taken power in the large cities of central Russia. But resistance developed in many other parts of the country. The "Whites," or anticommunists, had moved quickly to organize armies to fight the "Reds," or Communists. By 1920 most of the fighting was over. The Whites had been defeated.

The Union of Soviet Socialist Republics (USSR)

Russian Civil War:
White Army soldiers

In 1922 Russia became the Union of Soviet Socialist Republics. By then, Lenin had put the Communists firmly in charge. He had organized a strong police force. Every day the police arrested, jailed, and even killed enemies of communism. The police force often made their arrests at night, secretly. Many members of the clergy were arrested. Communists believed that religion was in the way. Religion misguided people, the Communists said.

Members of the nobility and of the middle class were labeled enemies of the state. They were arrested, jailed, and shot. The government took their businesses. Lenin and his secret police ruled by fear.

The Bolshevik Revolution was supposed to help the peasants. Now Lenin ordered farmers to turn their crops over to the government. Some farmers rebelled. There was more fighting. Throughout the early 1920s, the Communists struggled to maintain power. For a brief period, the Communists let up on their hold over factories and farms in order to win support.

Then, in 1924 Lenin became ill and died. He is remembered as the "Father of the Revolution." After his death, the Communists began a new struggle for leadership of the government.

Vladimir Ilyich Lenin

Joseph Stalin

Joseph Stalin was born in 1879 in what is now the Soviet republic of Georgia. He was educated in a religious school. His mother wanted him to become a priest. Then Joseph Stalin read the works of Karl Marx. "There is no God!" he announced at age 13. When he grew up, he became a revolutionary and then a leader in the Communist party.

Stalin's real name was Dzhugashvili. But in 1913, he adopted the name "Stalin," which means "man of iron" in Russian. Stalin took power after Lenin's death. He ruled the Soviet Union from 1924 until his death in 1953. He built up Russia's economy and industry. Stalin saw to the building of new factories and more heavy machinery. The peasants were forced to work on **collective** farms. He insisted that farmers use the new government machines. But he did not teach the farmers how to operate them. Farm production went down. There were food shortages again.

Joseph Stalin

Stalin made himself strong by destroying anyone who opposed him. Suspected enemies were shot or exiled to Siberia. People learned to be loyal to the Communist party and to Stalin.

Many people were unhappy living under such a tyrant. Stalin made life especially hard for Russian Jews. There were food shortages throughout the country. And certain goods, like clothing, were also hard to come by.

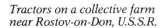
Tractors on a collective farm near Rostov-on-Don, U.S.S.R.

Russian newspapers and radio programs told nothing of the country's problems. Sources of news said only what Stalin wanted them to say. And Stalin would **censor** any news that came in from the rest of the world. Stalin did not allow Russians to travel outside the Soviet Union. For this reason, the Soviet Union was said to be surrounded by an "iron curtain."

Stalin had statues of himself put up all over Russia. He insisted that the statues be built to make him look taller and more handsome than he really was. Stalin actually rewrote Russian history. He tried to make it sound as if the Russian people had actually chosen him to be their leader.

Russia has a long history of being ruled by tyrants. Ivan the Terrible, Peter the Great, and many other czars were ruthless dictators. But many people think that Stalin was the most destructive and tyrannical dictator of all.

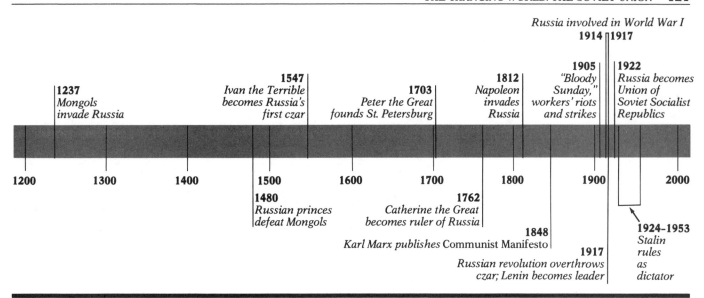

Timeline:

1237 — Mongols invade Russia
1480 — Russian princes defeat Mongols
1547 — Ivan the Terrible becomes Russia's first czar
1703 — Peter the Great founds St. Petersburg
1762 — Catherine the Great becomes ruler of Russia
1812 — Napoleon invades Russia
1848 — Karl Marx publishes *Communist Manifesto*
1905 — "Bloody Sunday," workers' riots and strikes
1914 — Russia involved in World War I
1917 — Russian revolution overthrows czar; Lenin becomes leader
1922 — Russia becomes Union of Soviet Socialist Republics
1924–1953 — Stalin rules as dictator

Timeline axis: 1200, 1300, 1400, 1500, 1600, 1700, 1800, 1900, 2000

Points to Remember

♦ The Soviet Union takes in a huge area; it is home to many types of people.

♦ Russian czars held power after 200 years of Mongol rule.

♦ Ivan the Terrible, who ruled by terror, was the first czar.

♦ Peter the Great gained land for Russia and opened a "window" to the rest of Europe. He westernized his country.

♦ Catherine the Great continued Peter's policies. The nobles of Russia were well educated and cultured, while the peasants grew poorer and poorer.

♦ Bloody Sunday, in 1905, began a revolt of the Russian workers.

♦ Czar Nicholas II led Russia into World War I in 1914. The war caused food shortages and was unpopular.

♦ In 1917 Nicholas II was overthrown. Later that year the Bolsheviks seized control of the government.

♦ The Bolsheviks, who followed the communist ideas of the German philosopher Karl Marx, supported Lenin as head of Russia's government.

♦ In 1922 Russia became known as the Union of Soviet Socialist Republics.

♦ Joseph Stalin followed Lenin as leader of the Communist party and of the Soviet Union.

Think About It!

1. What was life like for peasants, workers, and common people throughout most of Russia's history?

2. What were Lenin's ideals for a communist state? How did Lenin's ideas of communism differ from Marx's?

3. Describe the work of Lenin's secret police. Whom did they arrest?

4. What happened to religion under the Communists? To agriculture? To the middle class?

5. What kind of leader was Joseph Stalin?

6. What was the "iron curtain"?

Chapter 13

World War II

Words to Know

anti-Semitism   prejudice against Jews

concentration camps   prison camps for people thought to be dangerous to a ruling group

depressions   periods of low business activity and high unemployment

fascists   dictators and their followers who take away rights of the people and glorify war

genocide   an attempt to kill all the people of a certain race or religious group

Holocaust   the killing of millions of Jews by Germany's Nazis

pact   an agreement

resistance   a force opposing or working against something

scapegoat   a person or group blamed for the mistakes and problems of others

Look for the answers as you read:

1. Who were the dangerous dictators in power before World War II?

2. What did Germany do that helped to bring about World War II?

3. Who were the Allied powers and the Axis powers?

4. What happened to Hitler's plans to take over the Soviet Union?

5. How and when did the United States become involved in the war?

6. What kind of world did Hitler hope to build?

7. What was the Holocaust?

8. How did the war finally end in Europe? In Japan?

9. Why was the United Nations set up?

After World War I the League of Nations hoped to act as a peace-keeper. World War I had been costly in lives and in money. No one was anxious for another war. Yet only 20 years after World War I ended, another war began.

The 20 years between World War I and World War II were troubled years. In the early 1930s, nations struggled through **depressions**. Businesses went broke. Millions of workers were out of jobs. Farmers could not sell crops to unemployed people. Banks closed. Poverty spread throughout the world. Historians would call the 1930s the "Great Depression."

There were other troubles, too. In India, people were fighting for freedom from British rule. Civil wars were raging in China and Spain. And Japan was attacking China as part of its plan to build a large empire.

The Rise of Dictators

The years between World War I and World War II brought new governments to several nations. They were governments ruled by dictators. The Great Depression created a perfect climate for the rise of dictators. Hungry, hopeless people want to see changes. They are often ready to turn to a strong leader who promises a better future. Most of the dictators, however, were evil men who wanted power and control.

Mussolini

A man named Benito Mussolini took control of Italy in 1922. His followers were called **Fascists**. Mussolini won favor with his people by building roads and factories. "He made the trains run on time," people said. He improved his country's economy and industry, but insisted on absolute rule. Anyone who refused to obey Mussolini was jailed or killed.

Mussolini wanted Italy to become a great empire. He wanted to win colonies, to make war, and to take new lands by force. In 1935 Mussolini sent troops into Ethiopia, a free African country. The League of Nations protested. But it could not stop Mussolini's drive into Africa.

Benito Mussolini

Tojo

Hideki Tojo

In Japan, General Hideki Tojo arose as a dictator. He wanted to build an empire in Asia. Under the leadership of Tojo and other generals, Japanese forces invaded the Chinese province of Manchuria in 1931. When the League of Nations protested, Japan left the League. By 1932 Japan had claimed Manchuria. Japan invaded China again in 1937, taking over miles of coastal lands. By 1938 Japan controlled all of China's major ports and industrial centers. During the 1930s Japanese military officers began taking over their own government. Anyone who got in their way or protested was either jailed or assassinated. By 1940 Tojo had become Minister of War. And in 1941 he became Premier. Japan still had an emperor. But the emperor had no real power.

Hitler

The country that was most willing to accept a dictator and to follow him without question was Germany. Germany had suffered greatly after World War I. German pride had been crushed. A country whose nationalistic spirit was based on military greatness had been beaten in war. German armies had been reduced to almost nothing. And the Treaty of Versailles had forbidden the rebuilding of the German military.

The German economy was in a terrible state. The Great Depression hit hard, and Germany still had war debts to pay. Germans were out of work and hungry. They were angry and they were ready for revenge.

This situation in Germany led people to accept Adolf Hitler as their leader in 1933. Hitler was the head of the National Socialist, or Nazi, party. Hitler and the Nazis seemed to have an answer to Germany's problems. Hitler appealed to the Germans' wounded pride. He told them that they were a "super race" who should rule the world. He promised to return Germany to a position of power and glory.

Hitler spoke of winning back Germany's lost lands. He promised a new German empire, the Third Reich. In 1935 Hitler began building Germany's armed forces again. This had been forbidden by the Treaty of Versailles. But nothing was done to stop the Nazis from arming themselves.

As Hitler gave Germany new hope and national pride, he built his own strength. No one dared speak out against Adolf Hitler!

Adolf Hitler

Hitler strove to bind his people together with the feeling of hatred. He aimed that hate at all people who were not white and Germanic. Hitler believed that the German race was stronger, better, and smarter than any other. He gave fiery speeches that stirred German emotions. He told the people that Germans should be "masters of the world."

Hitler directed his fiercest hatred at the Jewish people. He encouraged **anti-Semitism**, a mindless hatred of Jews. He told the German people that the Jews were the cause of all their troubles. Hitler's lies gave the unhappy Germans a **scapegoat**. Now they had a simple way to explain away their troubles: they blamed them all on the Jews.

Hitler united Germany under a banner of hatred and fear. He made people afraid to disobey him. Hitler's secret police backed his rule. They arrested anyone who spoke against him. **Concentration camps** were built to imprison Hitler's enemies.

Hitler won Germany's loyalty. Then he turned to the rest of Europe. "Today Europe," Hitler declared, "tomorrow the world!"

Hitler's Weapon: Hate

The Axis

The three dictators—Hitler, Mussolini, and Tojo—each wanted an empire. In 1936 Hitler and Mussolini joined forces. They called their alliance the Rome–Berlin Axis. They chose the name "axis" to suggest that all of Europe revolved around Germany and Italy. In 1940 Japan joined the Axis. Germany, Italy, and Japan planned to conquer the world and divide it up!

World War II Begins

In 1938 Hitler set forth on his conquest of the world. His troops marched into Austria and took over the country. Austria was now a part of Germany.

"This is wrong," said Great Britain and France. "Hitler has broken the Treaty of Versailles." But they did not act to stop him.

Next Hitler turned to Czechoslovakia. Hitler claimed that Germans living there were treated poorly. He asked for a border region in Czechoslovakia. He said that this would be his last request for territory. Great Britain and France had sworn to protect Czechoslovakia. But, to keep peace, they signed a treaty with Hitler. They gave him 11,000 square miles of Czech lands. This area was known as the Sudetenland. Six months later, Hitler took over the rest of Czechoslovakia. The British and French policy of trying to satisfy Hitler by giving in had not worked.

On September 1, 1939, German armies invaded Poland. This time Great Britain and France acted. On September 3, 1939, they declared war on Germany. World War II had begun.

Hitler's *Blitzkrieg*

The German army took Poland in less than a month. Then Hitler pushed west. Norway and Denmark fell to Germany, too.

Hitler's style of warfare was called a *Blitzkrieg*, which means "lightning war." His armies moved fast, using quick attacks with planes, with tanks, and with troops. The people of Europe would remember the German planes bombing railroads, highways, and cities. They would remember the armored cars moving in next, followed by the Nazi foot soldiers.

The German *Blitzkrieg* then fell upon Holland, Luxembourg, and Belgium. Next came France.

France Falls

When the Germans attacked France, they had some help from Italy. France's armies were unable to stop Hitler. With Germans at the gates of Paris and with Nazi planes overhead, the French surrendered. In June 1940 the French admitted their defeat. It is said that Hitler received the news of France's surrender with great joy. He was so happy, in fact, that he danced a little "victory jig."

The Battle of Britain

With the fall of France, only Britain remained in Hitler's way. Hitler decided not to attack the island of Great Britain by sea. Britain's navy was too powerful. Hitler would launch an air attack instead.

The Battle of Britain was the first major air war in history. More than 1,000 German planes attacked Britain. They bombed cities and airfields. But the British would not be defeated. Britain's prime minister, Winston Churchill, was a strong leader. He declared, "We shall defend our island whatever the cost may be. . . . We shall never surrender!"

Bombing damage in London

British civilians worked out air raid plans to protect their neighborhoods. Citizens even strung piano wire from balloons to catch Nazi planes. The British Royal Air Force (RAF) fought back. They were skilled young pilots. With speedy Spitfire planes and with newly developed radar, they fought off the German planes.

Germany had to give up plans for a second attack on Britain. It was Germany's first defeat in World War II.

Hitler Moves East

Unable to take Britain, Hitler's armies moved eastward. The Germans took Romania and its oil fields. Then Italy invaded Greece. Greece's armies fought bravely against the Italians. But when Hitler joined the Italians, Greece had to surrender.

Next the Axis nations took Hungary, Bulgaria, and Yugoslavia. Most of Europe had now fallen under Hitler.

World War II in Europe

Hitler Turns on the Soviet Union

Like Napoleon Bonaparte, Hitler was out to conquer the world. Like Napoleon Bonaparte, Hitler chose June 22 as the day to attack Russia. Napoleon had attacked on June 22, 1812. Now Hitler attacked on June 22, 1941, with three million German soldiers. He expected Russia to fall in a matter of weeks.

But the Russians surprised the world by fighting back with amazing strength and determination. Soldiers and civilians alike stood up against the Germans. But the Germans advanced toward Moscow. Just as in the fight against Napoleon, Russians burned whatever they could not move. They destroyed food supplies, machinery, and factories. The Germans approached Moscow, but they were unable to take the city.

Like Napoleon, Hitler did not count on the fierce Russian weather. Hitler's soldiers did not even have winter clothing. And the winter of 1941–1942 turned out to be the worst in years. Nazi soldiers froze on the icy Russian plains. It was beginning to look as if Hitler might have made a mistake by invading Russia.

The Holocaust

Hitler forced his own ideas on the peoples he conquered. They were evil ideas of a "super race." White, Christian Europeans would be treated fairly well. But people who did not fit that mold were considered inferior. They were used as slave laborers or thrown into concentration camps.

Some Europeans fought the Nazi ideas. They formed **resistance** groups and waged secret, undercover wars. They wrecked telephone and telegraph lines to stop German communication. They blew up bridges and derailed trains. They killed Nazi officers. They helped Allied prisoners escape.

The Nazis answered the resistance by murdering hundreds of innocent men, women, and children. Nazi terror was aimed most directly at Europe's Jews. First Hitler forced Jews out of their jobs. He took their businesses and their property. Then Jews were made to live in special areas.

In 1941 Hitler's plans reached their evil peak. He announced his "final solution" to the "Jewish problem." That solution was **genocide**.

Hitler sent millions of Jews to concentration camps. Worse than any prison, the concentration camps were really death camps. There Jews were starved, lined up and shot, or gassed. Men were killed. Women were killed. Children were killed. Giant furnaces sent plumes of dark smoke into the sky as the prisoners' bodies were burned.

Jewish victims of Nazi persecution,
Warsaw Ghetto

Over six million Jews died in Nazi concentration camps. Hitler's efforts to destroy all Jews is called the **Holocaust**. The Nazis also murdered millions of others—Russians, Poles, Gypsies, Slavs—all "inferior" enemies of Hitler.

The Nazi death camps are one of history's greatest horrors. "How could the world have let this happen?" question the ghosts of Hitler's victims. Survivors of the Holocaust tell of wishing for death in a world too evil to bear.

The United States Declares War

The United States was a neutral nation from 1939 until 1941. It was not directly involved in the war.

The United States did, however, send aid to Germany's enemies. The United States sent food, arms, and raw materials to England and Russia. But it took a direct blow from Japan to bring the United States into World War II.

Japan was trying to create its empire in Asia. Japan felt that the United States stood in the way of control of the Pacific Ocean. On December 7, 1941, Japanese planes bombed the Pearl Harbor naval base in Hawaii. The attack took the United States by surprise. Almost one-half of the U.S. naval fleet was destroyed. Nearly 2,500 U.S. soldiers, sailors, and civilians died in the surprise attack.

In Japan, Emperor Hirohito declared war on the United States.

In America, President Franklin D. Roosevelt asked Congress to declare war on Japan. After a vote in Congress, Roosevelt addressed the nation. "We are now in this war," he declared. "We are in it all the way. . . ."

Three days later, Germany and Italy honored their **pact** with Japan. They declared war on the United States.

By the end of 1941, the war really had become a world war. The Axis countries stood on one side. The Allied countries, which now included the United States, stood on the other.

Wreckage of the U.S.S. Arizona *after bombing of Pearl Harbor*

The Tide of War Turns Toward the Allies

In 1942 Russian and German armies were locked in battle. The battle front stretched about 2,000 miles across Russia, from the Arctic to the Black Sea. In September of that year, the German Sixth Army attacked Stalingrad (now called Volgograd). For five months, Russian soldiers fought the Germans. The battle raged back and forth from one block to the next. Finally, on January 31, 1943, the German Sixth Army surrendered. Only 90,000 of the original force of 350,000 German soldiers were still alive.

The Battle of Stalingrad marked a major turning point in the war. Now the Russian army went on the offensive. The Russians began to take back cities that had been captured by the Germans.

Meanwhile, fighting had been going on in northern Africa. Hitler had taken over most of Europe. Now he could be attacked only from Britain, the Soviet Union, or from North Africa. North Africa became important.

General Erwin Rommel, known as the clever "Desert Fox," led the Germans in Africa. Early in 1943, America's General Dwight D. Eisenhower set a trap for the Desert Fox and defeated the Germans. In May of 1943, German and Italian forces in Africa surrendered.

The Allies invaded Italy next. It was, according to President Roosevelt, the "beginning of the end" for the Axis countries. The Allies accepted the Italian surrender in 1943. And Rome was freed on June 4, 1944.

The Invasion of Europe

Hitler still felt sure of his strength in Europe. But the Allies were preparing an invasion. By 1944 they were ready to attack France.

German forces protected the Normandy coast facing Great Britain. The Allies planned to invade Normandy. The day of the invasion was called "D-day."

D-day came at 2 A.M. on June 6, 1944. General Eisenhower was in charge of the attack. The first wave of troops crossed the English Channel. By 6:30 A.M. more than 150,000 Allied soldiers waded ashore on the beaches of Normandy. Within five days, the Allies had taken 80 miles of the coast.

The Allies began their sweep through France. In August they freed Paris. By October the Nazis were driven from all of France, as well as from Belgium and Luxembourg.

D-Day: American troops wading ashore at Normandy

Germany Surrenders

The Germans were soundly defeated in December 1944 in the Battle of the Bulge. According to Winston Churchill, it was the greatest American victory of the war.

At last the Allies invaded Germany, early in 1945. Germany's capital, Berlin, fell on May 2. On May 7, 1945, Germany surrendered. The war in Europe was over.

Death of the Dictators

What of the leaders of those fallen powers?

In Italy, Fascist leader Benito Mussolini met an ugly end. Mussolini tried to escape from Italy, to run from the antifascists. When he was captured, he begged for his life.

But Mussolini was executed—shot without a trial. His body was hung upside down outside a gas station in Milan, Italy. Italians shouted at the dictator's body, kicking it and throwing stones at it. A man who had lived by cruelty and terror met a cruel end.

Germany's Hitler died two days later. On April 30, 1945, reports came that the dictator had killed himself. He had been hiding in a bomb shelter beneath the flaming, shattered city of Berlin. Unable to face defeat, Hitler shot his new bride, Eva Braun, and then shot himself.

The War with Japan

The war had ended in Europe, but not in the Pacific. After Pearl Harbor, the Japanese had taken the Philippines, most of Southeast Asia, and islands in the Pacific.

General Douglas MacArthur led the U.S. forces against the Japanese in the Pacific. Although his campaigns were successful, the Japanese would not give up. Most of Japan's navy and air force had been destroyed by August of 1945. But there was no surrender. The Japanese felt it was their duty and their honor to fight to the very end.

The Japanese turned to desperate measures. "Kamikaze" pilots became human bombs. They did this by strapping themselves into planes filled with explosives. Then they flew their planes into American warships.

It was time for the terrors of war to end.

The U.S.S. Bunker Hill *after being struck by two Japanese suicide dive bombers*

Mushroom cloud from atomic bombing of Nagasaki

The Atom Bomb

Scientists had discovered how to split the atom to create great energy. Nations at war decided to use this energy as a weapon. They planned to build an atomic bomb. Throughout World War II, the Allies and the Axis nations had been racing to create such a bomb. Working on the project in America were scientists such as Enrico Fermi and J. Robert Oppenheimer. They, with the help of many others, finally built the powerful weapon.

U.S. president Harry S Truman made the difficult decision. The atomic bomb would be the quickest way to end the war.

Japan was warned. But the Japanese refused to surrender. So on August 6, 1945, an American plane dropped the atomic bomb on Hiroshima, Japan. In seconds, more than 90,000 people were killed, and Hiroshima was gone.

*Hiroshima after explosion
of atomic bomb*

Still, Japan did not surrender. So three days later, a second A-bomb was dropped on Nagasaki's 250,000 people.

At last, on September 2, 1945, the Japanese surrendered. It was their first military defeat in 2,000 years. General Tojo was arrested and convicted as a war criminal. He was hanged on December 23, 1948.

The Costs of War

World War II was over at last. It was the most expensive war in history. The figures were shocking:

- Over a trillion dollars had been spent for arms and war machinery.
- Fifty-five million lives were lost. (This includes civilian and military losses.)
- Germany lost almost three million soldiers.
- Japan lost more than two million soldiers.
- Italy lost about 160,000 soldiers.
- Russia lost about 7,500,000 soldiers.
- Britain lost about 270,000 soldiers.
- The United States lost more than 400,000 soldiers.
- France lost about 200,000 soldiers.

The world was left with questions to answer. How could people have so easily accepted the horrors of the Nazi concentration camps? And what about the atom bomb? What was to become of a world that possessed such a terrible and powerful weapon?

American tanks passing through Coutances, France

The United Nations

Following World War II, representatives of 50 nations gathered in San Francisco. They wanted to find a way to protect world peace.

The League of Nations had tried to keep the peace after World War I. But the League had failed. The 1945 meeting in San Francisco resulted in a new organization. It was called the United Nations. Its aim was to safeguard human rights throughout the world. The United States was the first nation to sign the U.N. charter.

United Nations headquarters, New York City

Whenever a world problem comes up, the United Nations meets to work for a peaceful settlement. Delegates from every member nation attend meetings of the United Nation's General Assembly. They try to solve problems without war. Other branches of the United Nations work on problems of education, trade, labor, health, and economics.

The weapons of the world have grown to unbelievable destructive power. The purpose of the United Nations has become more and more important. The United Nations has one victory as its major goal—the victory over war.

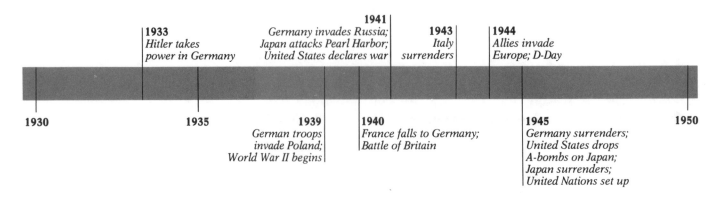

1933
Hitler takes power in Germany

1941
Germany invades Russia; Japan attacks Pearl Harbor; United States declares war

1943
Italy surrenders

1944
Allies invade Europe; D-Day

1930   1935

1939
German troops invade Poland; World War II begins

1940
France falls to Germany; Battle of Britain

1945   1950

1945
Germany surrenders; United States drops A-bombs on Japan; Japan surrenders; United Nations set up

Points to Remember

♦ Three strong dictators took power before World War II. They were Mussolini of Italy, General Tojo of Japan, and Hitler of Germany. Each wanted to build an empire.

♦ Hitler convinced the German people that they were members of a "super race" meant to rule the world.

♦ Germany, Italy, and Japan joined together as the Axis nations. The nations who would fight against them were called the Allied nations. The Allies included Britain, France, Russia, and the United States, as well as many smaller nations.

♦ Hitler's armies swept through Europe with a style of lightning warfare known as a *Blitzkrieg*.

♦ Germans took France but were unable to defeat Great Britain. Hitler tried to take the Soviet Union but failed.

♦ Hitler hated the Jews and tried to destroy them. In the Holocaust he imprisoned Jews in concentration camps where millions were murdered.

♦ The United States joined World War II in December 1941, after the Japanese bombed Pearl Harbor.

♦ The Invasion of Normandy on D-Day, June 6, 1944, began the Allied sweep to regain Europe.

♦ Germany surrendered on May 7, 1945, after Berlin fell to the Allies.

♦ War with Japan ended on September 2, 1945, after the United States dropped atomic bombs on Hiroshima and Nagasaki. It was the first use of atomic power in war.

♦ Nations of the world set up the United Nations as a peace-keeping organization.

Think About It!

1. How did the Great Depression contribute to the rise of dictators?

2. What is fascism?

3. Describe Hitler's ideas, the world he hoped to build, and the methods he used.

4. Which nation lost the most soldiers in World War II?

5. How was the World War II experience different for the people of Britain and for the people of the United States?

6. How did the dropping of the A-bomb on Japan in 1945 change the world? Why did the A-bomb make the United Nations so necessary?

Chapter 14

The Postwar World

Words to Know

apartheid   the separation of races based mainly on skin color

brainwashed   trained to have a whole new set of ideas and beliefs

capitalist   having business and industry privately owned and operated for profit

commune   a group of people working or living closely together, often sharing property and tasks

corrupt   dishonest, evil, selfish

curfews   times after which certain people cannot be on the streets

domino   a small, rectangular piece of wood or plastic used in a game; one side of the piece is either blank or marked with dots

guerilla   one of a group of fighters who are not part of a regular army, and who usually make surprise raids behind enemy lines

majority   a greater number, more than half

minority   a smaller number, less than half

oppressed   kept down by harsh rule

pollution   waste materials in the air or water

recognize   to accept the government of a country and deal with it in business and trade

refugees   those who flee their country or home

sanctions   actions taken by one nation against another for breaking international law; for example, a shipping blockade

satellites   countries that depend on and are controlled by a more powerful country

Look for the answers as you read:

1. What was the Marshall Plan?

2. How was Germany divided after World War II?

3. What is the "cold war"? What is NATO? What is the Warsaw Pact?

4. What changes in the Soviet Union is Mikhail Gorbachev responsible for?

5. What problems does India face today?

6. How did Mao Tse-tung and the Communists take over China?

7. What led to war in Korea?

8. How did Japan develop into a strong, industrial nation after World War II?

9. Why did the United States become involved in the conflict in Vietnam? How did the Vietnam War end?

10. What problems do African nations face today?

Europe was weakened by World War II. European countries were no longer the powerful nations they had been. It was time for these nations to rebuild.

U.S. president Harry S Truman called for a plan to help put Europe back on its feet. The Marshall Plan, named for U.S. secretary of state George C. Marshall, provided money for European recovery. From 1947 until 1951, the United States gave aid to European nations. Thirteen billion dollars worth of food, raw materials for industry, and machinery were sent to Europe.

War-torn nations welcomed the aid. But the Soviet Union and its communist **satellites** refused to accept the Marshall Plan. This refusal was just one act that divided the world into two camps.

The Marshall Plan

After World War II, many European nations rebuilt democratic governments. France had enjoyed a democracy known as the Third Republic before World War II. Then Germany took over the country. After the war, France returned to its democracy. It set up the Fourth Republic and then the Fifth Republic. Charles de Gaulle served as the first president of the postwar republics.

Italy was not anxious to return to a monarchy after its experience with Mussolini. So Italians set up a democratic government with a parliament and free elections.

The Eastern European countries did not turn to democracy. They became communist satellites of the Soviet Union. They had been freed from the Germans by the Soviet Union at the end of the war. But they remained under Soviet control.

Democracy in Europe

What of the defeated empire? Germany was a shambles after World War II. Cities and farms had been bombed. The economy was ruined.

Leaders of the winning nations met to decide Germany's fate. They divided Germany into four sections. Great Britain, France, the United States, and the Soviet Union each took control of a section. Each country put troops inside its zone to keep order.

After a few years the United States, France, and Britain tried to bring Germany together as one republic. But the Soviet Union refused. So the democratic nations combined their regions to form West Germany. The Soviet-controlled zone became known as East Germany. It still remains a communist nation.

Germany After the War

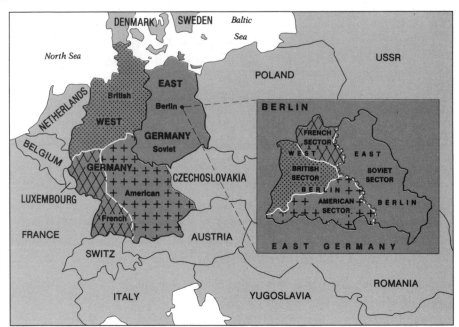

The division of Germany after World War II

A City Divided

Berlin, the capital of West Germany, is located in East Germany. That city was divided into East Berlin, a communist section, and West Berlin, under democratic West German control. In 1961 the Communists built the Berlin Wall. They wanted to separate the city's two sections. They also wanted to keep East Berliners from escaping to the West. Just two years after the wall was built, 16,456 people had escaped into West Berlin.

Building the Berlin Wall

Germany Today

Today Germany is still two separate countries. East Germany, called the German Democratic Republic, is a communist country. The people have little individual freedom. The government keeps tight control. West Germany is called the Federal Republic of Germany. It is a democracy with a parliament and elected representatives. West Germany has a chancellor at the head of its government. Konrad Adenauer was the first chancellor of West Germany.

World War II put an end to the old German tradition of militarism. The ideas of people like Bismarck and Hitler no longer push Germans to be conquerors. West Germany maintains an army. But it makes no moves of aggression. And it is nothing like it was under Hitler's Nazis.

Industry has grown in Germany since World War II. Many people, especially skilled workers and professional people, fled East Germany to live in West Germany. Because of this, the West German economy has improved rapidly.

The United States After World War II

The United States, unlike Europe, was not shattered by World War II. No battlefields tore apart U.S. lands. Wide oceans kept the United States separate and safe. The United States also had the power of the atomic bomb. At the end of World War II, the United States was the strongest nation in the world.

Except for its involvement in World War I, the United States had always kept to its own business. It followed a policy of isolationism. World War II connected the United States with the rest of the world. In 1945 the United States became one of the first countries to join the United Nations. The world was changing. Countries were becoming more and more dependent on each other. The United States could no longer stand alone, minding its own business.

U.S. Relations with the Soviet Union: The Cold War

During the world wars, the United States and the Soviet Union were allies. After World War II, the two countries became the most powerful nations on earth. In fact, they are known as "superpowers." Each had different ideas about what an ideal society should be like. Soviet peoples lived under communism, while Americans lived in a free democracy. Disputes and tensions between the two nations grew. The "cold war" had begun.

A cold war is not an outright conflict. It doesn't involve actual battles or bombings. A cold war is a war of ideas.

Both the Soviet Union and the United States have their own allies in the cold war. The United States and its allies say that communism is bad. They point out that people in communist countries usually have little freedom. The communist nations criticize the United States for being a **capitalist** nation. They point out that some people in the United States are very rich and some are very poor. They say that because of this, the United States is a very unfair society.

The United States Fights Communism

Americans worried about a communist takeover of the whole world.

U.S. president Harry S Truman announced that America would give aid to any country fighting communism. He made a plan for military and economic support. This plan became known as the Truman Doctrine. Both Greece and Turkey were given aid under this plan.

Communism often grows strong in poor countries. So the Marshall Plan fought communism, too. Financial aid under the Marshall Plan kept the European nations strong enough to resist communist ideas.

NATO

In 1950 sides were clearly drawn in the cold war. The United States led the setting up of the North Atlantic Treaty Organization (NATO). Members of NATO included the United States, Britain, France, Italy, Canada, and several smaller nations. In 1954 West Germany became a member.

NATO began as a defense against communism. Member nations promised to help each other. They said that an attack against any one of them would be taken as an attack against all.

In 1955 the Soviet Union created its own alliance to balance the NATO alliance. It was called the Warsaw Pact. It included the Soviet Union and its communist allies in Eastern Europe.

The Soviet Union and the United States try to stay in step with each other. Each superpower fears that the other will become more powerful.

One measure of power is the buildup of weapons. When the United States exploded the atom bomb in 1945, it made America more fearsome and powerful. Other nations wanted that power, too. In 1949 the Soviet Union exploded its first atomic bomb. By 1952 Great Britain also had the atomic secret. Then the United States pulled ahead again in the race for destructive power. In 1954 the U.S. tested a hydrogen bomb. It was thousands of times more powerful than the atomic bomb that had fallen on Hiroshima. Soon Great Britain, France, and the Soviet Union had hydrogen bombs, too.

Now the People's Republic of China has the bomb. So does India. The world has given itself something to fear. As nations struggle to keep pace in the cold war, the stakes become higher. Each superpower now has enough nuclear weapons to destroy the world many times over.

The Cold War Means a Race to Stay Ahead

During World War II, Joseph Stalin was the Soviet leader. After the war Stalin worked to rebuild Soviet industry. He set up labor camps, forcing workers to build, build, and build some more. Between 1945 and 1965, Soviet industry boomed. But life was not easy for the Russian worker.

Before World War II, most of the Eastern European countries had agricultural economies. After the war the Communists encouraged industry in the satellite nations. They took many farmers from their fields and put them to work in government factories.

The Soviet Union After World War II

Stalin died in 1953. He did not leave a good situation in the Soviet Union. During the last years of his leadership, he had taken many personal freedoms away from the people. He had persecuted Soviet Jews and encouraged extreme prejudice against them. He had created food shortages and clothing shortages with his emphasis on heavy industry.

Khrushchev Leads the Soviet Union

Nikita Khrushchev

After Stalin's death, there was a struggle for power. Then a new leader, Nikita Khrushchev, rose to the top of the Communist party. Khrushchev criticized Stalin. He accused the former leader of the arrests and deaths of many citizens. Khrushchev promised that now the country would be led by the Party rather than by a single dictator.

Under Khrushchev life became better for the people of the Soviet Union. Khrushchev halted some of the activities of the secret police. The government allowed somewhat greater freedom of speech. The work week was shortened to 40 hours. And Khrushchev tried to raise the standard of living for ordinary people. His economic plan included a greater production of consumer goods. But progress was very slow.

Soviet Satellites

In 1948 Yugoslavia had succeeded in setting up its own government with aid from the Marshall Plan. Yugoslavia was still a communist country. But it was no longer under the Soviet thumb.

After Stalin's death some other countries of Eastern Europe tried to break from Soviet control. In 1956 Hungary tried to cut its ties with the Soviets. It wanted to set up its own communist government. But Soviet troops marched into Hungary, crushing the movement for independence.

Then in 1968 there was trouble in Czechoslovakia. The Soviet government felt that the Czechoslovakian Communist party was losing control of the country. The Russians were afraid that too much freedom of speech would turn the people away from communism. So in August of that year, Soviet tanks rumbled through the streets of Prague. Soon new people were running the government—people chosen by the Russians.

Lech Walesa (left)

In the 1970s workers rioted in Poland. They were demanding higher pay and better working conditions. They wanted a union, something unheard of under communist governments. In 1980 the Polish government allowed the workers to form the union. The new workers' union was called Solidarity.

In 1982 the government began to fear that Solidarity went against communist ideals. That year, the Communists arrested Solidarity's leaders and declared the union illegal. Many insisted that the Soviet Union was behind the breakup of the workers' union in Poland.

The Spread of Communism

Communism has spread to other parts of the world. China, Mongolia, North Korea, as well as some nations in Southeast Asia and in Africa, have turned to communism. And Cuba, only 90 miles from the United States, became a communist dictatorship under Fidel Castro.

The Soviet Union has aided the spread of communism. This has increased the tensions of the cold war. In 1962 the Soviets tried to build missile bases in Cuba. To stop Soviet ships, U.S. president John F. Kennedy set up a blockade around Cuba. The cold war nearly turned hot at that point. The Cuban missile crisis brought the world to the edge of another big war. But Khrushchev agreed to take the missiles out of Cuba, and the situation cooled.

In 1963 Khrushchev's farm program collapsed. Russia had to buy a huge quantity of grain from the West. That year Soviet industrialization slowed down. Then Khrushchev came under heavy criticism for the way he had handled the Cuban situation. In 1964 he was forced to retire. Leonid Brezhnev and Alexei Kosygin replaced him as leaders of the Communist party. Now life became worse for the people of the Soviet Union. Once again, people had to be very careful about what they said.

Peace Talks

Both the United States and the Soviet Union realize that another world war would bring disaster. Between the quarrels and the peaks of tension, they meet to try to solve their problems.

In 1963 the United States and the Soviet Union set up a "hot line." This is a special direct communications link between Moscow and Washington, D.C. It enables the leaders of both countries to contact each other instantly. The purpose is to prevent an international crisis from turning the cold war into a hot war.

*Richard Nixon and Leonid Brezhnev
signing the SALT agreement*

In 1972 the two powers held Strategic Arms Limitation Talks (SALT). They met to set some limits on nuclear arms. They understood that world peace was at stake.

A second SALT agreement was later proposed. SALT II was a treaty putting strict limits on the building of nuclear weapons. But the U.S. Congress did not approve SALT II. It was angered by the Soviet invasion of Afghanistan.

The cold war goes on. Tensions and conflicts continue to tear the world apart. But the Soviet Union and the United States know they must keep the peace.

In 1987 Soviet leader Mikhail Gorbachev and U.S. president Ronald Reagan signed the INF (Intermediate Nuclear Forces) treaty. For the first time, both sides agreed to get rid of an entire class of nuclear weapons. And in 1988 both countries were hoping to reach agreement on another treaty. The START (Strategic Arms Reduction Treaty) treaty would cut in half the number of nuclear weapons on both sides. Also in 1988, Gorbachev agreed to bring the Soviet troops home from Afghanistan.

Under Gorbachev there has been a real lessening of tensions between the superpowers. Gorbachev put into action his policy of *Glasnost* or "openness." Soviet citizens now have more freedom of speech than ever before.

Gorbachev knew that the Soviet economy was in big trouble. And he knew that he would have to make major changes in order to see any improvement. So he proposed a policy of *Perestroika,* or "restructuring." Factories and businesses around the country would no longer be controlled by Moscow. Each would be responsible for running its own operations. And individual Soviet citizens would be allowed to engage in small-scale private business.

Gorbachev also welcomed U.S. corporations to set up joint operations in the Soviet Union. A number of U.S. companies have already signed agreements with the Soviets. In Moscow a MacDonald's opened for business. And an American pizzamaker has also set up shop.

But in spite of all the changes taking place, there were questions in the minds of every Russian. Would Gorbachev's plans be successful? And what would happen if Gorbachev were to fall from power?

India After World War II: A Divided Nation

In 1947 India won independence from Britain. At that time, Indian leaders agreed to divide India into two separate nations, India and Pakistan. India fell under the control of the Hindus. And the Moslems controlled Pakistan. A further complication was the division of Pakistan into East and West Pakistan.

The division was not easily made. Hindus fled Pakistan. Moslems left India. There was fighting and confusion. Millions of Moslems still remained in India. There was more fighting. Thousands of Indians were killed.

Then Gandhi went on his hunger strike, refusing to eat until the violence ended. Gandhi's fast brought peace, but in 1948, Gandhi was killed by a Hindu assassin.

An Independent India

India held its first general election in 1951. Jawaharlal Nehru was elected as the first prime minister of the Republic of India. Nehru led India until he died in 1964. In 1966 his daughter, Indira Gandhi, was elected prime minister.

There were food shortages and labor strikes in India during Mrs. Gandhi's years as leader. For a time she lost her position. But she returned to power in 1980. Then in 1984, Indira Gandhi, too, was assassinated.

India's Borders

Over the years, India has had border disputes with its neighbors. This led to fighting between India and China in 1959 and in 1962.

In 1965 India and Pakistan fought a three-week-long war. Both countries claimed the same land, called Kashmir, in northern India.

In 1971 civil war broke out in Pakistan. The people of East Pakistan complained because the center of government was based in West Pakistan. The war led to East Pakistan becoming a separate nation called Bangladesh.

India's Problems

India has always had to deal with poverty and food shortages. The country has a huge population. And it must struggle to provide enough food for all its people. India is one of the world's larger producers of farm products. But there is never enough food to go around. It is said that almost two-thirds of India's people go to bed hungry every night.

Poverty in India: Homeless people

The government has tried to teach farmers new methods to increase production. They have allowed Western businesses to come in and build chemical factories. There was hope that the chemicals would increase crops. In general, India benefited from the chemicals. But in 1984, an accident at one U.S. chemical plant caused the worst industrial disaster in history. There was an explosion at the Union Carbide factory in Bhopal, India. A cloud of highly toxic gas spread into the heavily populated area surrounding the plant. Several thousand people who breathed the poisonous fumes died horrible deaths.

India is trying to combat its poverty with programs for economic growth. Indian leaders try to build industry. They want to make better use of their country's resources, such as coal and iron ore. And India spends billions of dollars building dams to provide power.

Age-old customs contribute to the food shortages. While India has tried to industrialize, most of its people still cling to old ideas. In 1950 the government tried to improve life by outlawing the "untouchable" category in the Hindu caste system. Until then, people called untouchables had been forced to live in the dirtiest, poorest parts of villages. Their children were not allowed to go into schools. They had to sit on the steps outside and listen. If an untouchable walked through village streets, he was supposed to wipe away his footsteps with a broom. Old ideas die hard. And India has had to move beyond some of those ideas to make life better for its people.

In China, Chiang Kai-shek and his Nationalist party had come to power in 1927. Some members of the Nationalist party believed in communism. The Communists felt that Chiang showed favor to rich landowners and businessmen. So the Communists broke away from the Nationalists. And in 1927 they took over the city of Shanghai.

China After World War II

Chiang expelled the Communists from the Nationalist party. A struggle began between Chinese Nationalists and Chinese Communists. Stalin and the Soviet Union supported the Communists. Stalin encouraged them to win support of China's factory workers.

But China's strength did not lay in the city workers. It lay in the farm peasants. A man named Mao Tse-tung, born a peasant, turned to the peasants for Communist strength.

Mao Tse-tung and the Communists

Mao Tse-tung

During World War II the Communists helped defend the peasants of northern China against the Japanese. Mao and the Communists won the peasants' loyalty.

After the war the Communists and Nationalists continued their struggle for China. There were four years of civil war. The Nationalists had better supplies and a larger army. But they no longer had the support of the people. Many Nationalist leaders were **corrupt**. They wanted to become rich themselves while the Chinese people went hungry. The Communists divided land and food fairly among the people. So they received the peasants' support.

By 1948 the war had turned in favor of the Communists. Chiang Kai-shek and the Nationalists decided it was time to get out. They left mainland China to live in Taiwan. In 1949 China was taken over by Mao Tse-tung and the Communists. They called their nation the People's Republic of China.

The Soviet Union was quick to **recognize** the new government. And so were many other nations. But the United States refused to recognize the Communist government.

The United States recognized the Nationalist government in Taiwan and supported it. Taiwan, calling itself the Republic of China, kept its seat in the United Nations. Until 1971 the United States kept the People's Republic of China out of the United Nations. In 1972 U.S. president Richard Nixon made an eight-day visit to the People's Republic. At the end of the visit, Nixon and the Chinese leaders issued a statement. They promised that both powers would work to bring about normal relations between the countries. In 1979 U.S. president Jimmy Carter finally recognized the People's Republic of China.

Communism in China

Team of peasants planning construction of hillside terraces, Huangtien Commune, China

One-fifth of the population of the world lives in China! Producing enough food to feed more than one billion people is no simple matter. The Communists knew they had to solve that problem. So they took land away from rich farmers. They set up huge farm **communes**. The peasants had to work on these communes. Sometimes as many as 10,000 people worked on a single commune. The government also took over industries, built new factories, and trained workers.

The Communists insisted on the support and loyalty of all the people. Workers had to attend meetings where they read aloud from Mao Tse-tung's writings. They talked about how Mao's ideas could make them better citizens of a better China.

The Cultural Revolution

Mao and the Communists worried that people might prefer the Old China to the New China. They held their communist meetings to teach people to think the communist way. Enemies of communism were punished. They were **brainwashed**, or forced to accept the communist way of thought.

For a while Mao's harsh policies worked. But from 1965 to 1968 there was a decline in China's economy. During this period, Mao called his policies a "Cultural Revolution." The Cultural Revolution was supposed to build loyalty for the Communists. Young students, called "Red Guards," became soldiers for communism. They helped Mao enforce his policies.

Farm production fell. Factory production fell. China closed its doors to visitors from the rest of the world. The Chinese leaders wanted to make sure that no anticommunist ideas could filter in.

A government official speaking to workers on a commune, Hainan Island, China

Soviet-Chinese Relations Decline; U.S.-Chinese Relations Improve

During the 1970s, relations between the United States and China improved. Meanwhile, relations between the Soviet Union and China grew worse. Their styles of communism were different. And they could not agree on many issues. Border disputes arose between the two communist giants. Several battles were fought between Soviet and Chinese army units. There were deaths on both sides. Suddenly, the rest of the world took notice of the tense situation. The Soviets had moved hundreds of thousands of troops to the border region. People began to wonder about the possibility of full-scale war between Russia and China. Fortunately it never came to that. Over time, relations between the two powers slowly improved.

After Mao's death in 1976, trade relations between China and the rest of the world improved. Under Deng Xiaoping and other leaders, China has been trying to modernize. The United States maintains good relations with both the Communist People's Republic and Nationalist Taiwan.

Conflict in Korea

Korea, with its northern border on China, became a hot spot in the world in 1950. Korea had been controlled by the Japanese during World War II. In 1945 the country was divided into two parts. North Korea had the support of Soviet Communists. South Korea had American support.

In 1950 North Korea suddenly attacked South Korea. The Communists threatened to take the whole country.

South Korea turned to the United Nations for help. A U.N. army made up mostly of American soldiers came to South Korea's aid. The U.N. troops and South Koreans pushed the Communists back, almost to the Chinese border. The Chinese began to worry. Then the Chinese Communists sent 780,000 soldiers to help North Korea.

The U.N.-South Korean troops fought the Chinese-North Korean troops for three years. In 1953 a truce was finally declared. The division between North and South Korea stayed exactly as it had been before the conflict began.

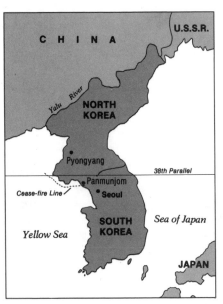

The Korean peninsula

The explosion of the atomic bomb left Japan reeling. Japan surrendered and World War II was over. Then the Allied forces occupied Japan. U.S. general Douglas MacArthur was the Supreme Commander. His job was to build a democracy in Japan.

A new democratic constitution was written in 1946. The constitution gave power to an elected prime minister. And it gave women the right to vote. Japan would be allowed to keep its emperor. But he would have no power. He would serve only as a symbol of the Japanese spirit. In 1951 the government was put back into the hands of the Japanese. The Allied occupation had ended.

Japan After World War II

The new Japanese constitution stated that Japan would not maintain a strong military. So the Japanese turned from a policy of war to one of industrial and economic growth.

Today Japan has become a world leader in industry. Japan is one of the world's largest steel producers. It is the second largest manufacturer of automobiles and electronics equipment. And it is a leading shipbuilder. This is quite an accomplishment since Japan has few natural resources of its own. The country's industrial success depends on trade, the import of raw materials, and the export of finished products.

Japan is a small, crowded country. There is little room to grow food. Again Japan depends on imports, bringing in at least 30 percent of its food. And Japan has had to combat problems caused by overcrowding, such as **pollution** and housing shortages. But Japan has made amazing progress. World War II had left Japan in ruins. But in less than 50 years, Japan has become a great economic and industrial power.

Industry in Japan

Japan took over much of Southeast Asia during World War II. Before the war all of the area, except Thailand, was colonized by European nations. After the war anticolonial feelings were strong. The nations of Southeast Asia wanted to be free.

Some countries gained independence easily. Others had to struggle.

Southeast Asia After World War II

The Philippines, a United States colony since 1898, was granted its freedom in 1935. The Japanese took the islands during World War II. But July 4, 1946, became Independence Day for the Republic of the Philippines.

The country of Burma, once held by Britain, gained independence peacefully in 1948.

The 13,600 islands that make up Indonesia freed themselves from Dutch rule through revolt. Indonesia gained its independence in 1949, after four years of bitter fighting.

In 1965 Singapore left the Malaysian Federation to form its own republic.

The new, independent republics all faced their own problems. In many, there were bitter civil struggles.

Conflict in Vietnam

The Vietnam War

In the 1800s France took over an area of Southeast Asia called Indochina. Indochina was made up of the countries of Vietnam, Laos, and Cambodia (now called Kampuchea). During World War II, Japan took Indochina from the French. Then France regained Indochina after the war.

But Indochina was not anxious to return to French rule. Nationalists and Communists had gained a foothold there.

In 1946 the fighting began. The Vietnamese Communists wanted to force the French out of the country. The French set up a government in the South. The Communists, under their leader, Ho Chi Minh, set up a government in the North. The Communists defeated the French in 1954. Then a conference in Geneva, Switzerland, decided what would happen next.

Representatives from France, the Vietnamese Communists, Cambodia, Laos, China, Britain, and the United States all came to that conference. They made their decision. Vietnam was divided into two zones. Ho Chi Minh and the Communists would continue to rule the North. South Vietnam was supposed to hold an election to choose its own form of government.

But a free election never took place. Ngo Dinh Diem took leadership and refused to hold elections. Meanwhile, North Vietnam grew stronger with the support of Communist China and the Soviet Union. The political situation in South Vietnam remained unsettled.

The Vietcong, Communist **guerilla** fighters, began an attempt to take over South Vietnam in 1957. In 1963 South Vietnam's leader, Diem, was assassinated. The country's problems increased. The government changed hands nine times in three years.

The United States Sends Help

The Soviet Union and China continued aid to North Vietnam. In the 1960s the U.S. government sent aid to South Vietnam because it believed in the **domino** theory. If dominoes are stood in a line together, the fall of one domino will knock down the others. The domino theory was the idea that if one country became communistic, neighbors would fall to the Communists, too.

At first the United States sent money and supplies. Then, in 1965 U.S. president Lyndon B. Johnson sent more than 3,500 U.S. marines to Da Nang, South Vietnam. They were the first United States combat troops to join the fight. Thousands more would follow. By 1969 there were more than 543,000 U.S. troops in Vietnam.

*A Vietnamese mother and children crossing a river
to escape the bombing of their village*

Americans Protest U.S. Involvement

Many Americans didn't want the United States to get into the war in Southeast Asia. When American soldiers began dying in Vietnamese jungles, the protests grew stronger. On May 15, 1966, more than 10,000 people picketed the White House in Washington, D.C., to protest U.S. involvement in the war. College students across the nation spoke out against the war. On May 13, 1967, more than 70,000 marchers paraded down New York City's 5th Avenue. And 250,000 people marched against the war in Washington D.C. on October 15, 1969.

"Bring home our troops!" they shouted. But the war went on. More and more Americans were killed and wounded. The Vietcong remained strong. There didn't seem to be any light at the end of the tunnel.

Anti-Vietnam War demonstration, Washington, D.C.

By the end of the decade, the United States was a nation in turmoil. The growing antiwar movement had helped to touch off a general youth protest movement. The middle-class youth of America were questioning and protesting against all the values of their parents.

Also during the 1960s, there had been a series of assassinations that had shocked the nation. President John F. Kennedy, in 1963, and his brother Robert F. Kennedy, in 1968, had been shot to death. So had black leaders Malcolm X, in 1965, and Martin Luther King, Jr., in 1968. This was the last straw for many blacks. In general, blacks were becoming angry and frustrated at not being able to share in the growing prosperity of white America. Now feeling that they had nothing to lose, they took their cause to the streets. Rioting occurred in many American cities.

National Guard on duty during riot in Detroit's Black ghetto

In 1973 the United States decided to take its troops out of Vietnam. About 58,000 Americans had been killed. About 365,000 had been wounded. And the war had not been won.

In general, the 1970s in the United States was a quieter time than the 1960s. However, one more great shock was in store for Americans. In 1972 a team of burglars had broken into Democratic headquarters in a building called the Watergate. They were caught. There was a long investigation. And the burglars proved to have been working for people in the White House. The White House attempted a cover-up. When the cover-up failed, President Richard Nixon had to resign from office in August 1974. He was the only president in the history of the United States to be forced out of office.

In 1975, Saigon, the capital of South Vietnam, fell to the Vietcong. The name of the city was changed to "Ho Chi Minh City." Vietnam was united as a communist country in 1976. Then the "dominoes" fell. Communists took power in Laos and Cambodia. And in 1978 Vietnam invaded Cambodia.

Refugees from Communism: The Boat People

Many people in Vietnam, Laos, and Cambodia did not want to live under communist rule. They fled their homelands. Many **refugees** escaped by boat. They became known as "boat people"—people who no longer had a home. A large number came to the United States. Some died making their escapes. All suffered hardships along their way. Crowded refugee camps housed those who had nowhere to go.

Vietnamese refugees

Africa After World War II

During the nineteenth century, Africa had been divided into European-ruled colonies. In 1945, at the end of World War II, most of Africa remained under European rule. Exceptions were the countries of South Africa, Ethiopia, Liberia, and Egypt. Many Africans had joined the armies of their European motherlands during the war. When they returned to Africa, they wanted independence.

The years after 1945 saw European colonies in Africa gain freedom, one by one. Some won their independence peacefully. For other nations, freedom came only through struggle and revolt.

Several colonies were ruled by the British. Most of these gained independence during the 1950s. Sudan, the largest nation in Africa, won freedom from Britain in 1956. And some of the free nations changed their names. When the Gold Coast won its freedom in 1957, it became Ghana.

Kenya was an African nation that had to struggle for independence from Britain. A rebellion by a group known as the Mau Mau lasted from 1952 until 1956. A man named Jomo Kenyatta was the leader of the Mau Mau. He was thrown in jail in 1953. Britain granted independence to Kenya in 1963. And Kenyatta became the leader of the new, free nation. He ruled Kenya until his death in 1978.

Freedom Brings New Problems

Freedom did not always mean an end to problems and unrest. The new nations had troubles of their own. Four different governments have held power in Ghana since its independence. Nigeria, freed in 1960, has seen civil war and a breakup of the new nation. In 1966 the eastern part of Nigeria separated and became a country called Biafra. This led to civil war. And with the war came starvation, disease, and death for nearly two million people.

Problems plagued Uganda when General Idi Amin took over the independent government in 1971. Amin saw to it that thousands of Ugandans were killed. Anyone against Amin died! Finally the people revolted. And in 1979 they forced Amin from power.

Rhodesia Wins Black Majority Rule

Independence did not bring an end to racial prejudice in some new African nations. Sometimes those nations had more problems with the new governments than with the European rulers. When Rhodesia gained independence from Britain in 1965, black Africans had no voice in government. A white **minority** ruled for 15 years.

Britain wanted blacks to have rights. But the new white rulers said no. Britain asked the United Nations to place **sanctions** on Rhodesia. Black revolutionaries began a guerilla war.

In 1980 Rhodesia's first black **majority** government finally came to power through a general election. The new government officially changed the nation's name. Rhodesia became Zimbabwe, an ancient African name for that part of the continent.

White Minority Still Rules South Africa

Of all the independent countries in Africa, only South Africa has a white minority still in complete power. The country is ruled by Afrikaners. These are the descendants of Dutch colonists who began settling in South Africa as early as 1652. The Afrikaners feel that the country belongs to them. They helped win South Africa's independence from Britain in 1910.

The Afrikaners wanted to keep white people in control. So in 1948, they set up their policy of **apartheid**, or separation of races. They passed laws to separate people according to race. By law, people of certain races can live, own property, or run businesses only in certain zones.

Black South African taking a chance by sitting on "Europeans only" bench

Curfews regulate the time black people must be off the streets of South Africa. Separate trains, beaches, schools, and other facilities are provided for blacks and whites. Laws do nothing to stop whites from getting the best facilities and blacks the worst.

Many people in South Africa and around the world are strongly against apartheid. But many South Africans who protest are arrested, and apartheid continues. A white minority still rules in South Africa.

South Africa has been involved in a struggle with its neighbor, Namibia, since 1915. In that year, South Africa took Namibia away from Germany. Ever since then, South Africa has tried to rule there. The United Nations has declared South Africa's rule of Namibia to be illegal. And black nationalists continue fighting to make Namibia free.

A country cannot be at peace when people are **oppressed**. South Africa is still a nation of unrest.

Algeria

Colonies in Africa also broke away from Portugal and France. By 1960 France had granted freedom to all its African colonies except Algeria. It took a violent revolution to free Algeria from French rule. More than 250,000 lives were lost in the fighting, which had begun in 1954. But Algerians finally won their independence in 1962. Today Algeria has a military government with strong ties to the Soviet Union.

Morocco, to the west of Algeria, is ruled by a king. Its government is friendly with the United States and with France. Morocco has tried to claim the Western Sahara. But Algerians oppose that claim, and there have been tensions between Soviet-supported Algeria and U.S.-supported Morocco.

Libya

Libya, once ruled by Italy, became a free nation in 1951. At first free Libya was ruled by a king. Then in 1969, Muammar al-Qadaffi and his followers overthrew the royal government. Qadaffi formed ties with the Soviet Union and broke off Libya's relations with Western nations.

Libya is considered important in today's world because it has many oil fields. Libya's Qadaffi has shown great interest in expanding his country's borders and increasing its power. He spends much of Libya's oil profits on new weapons and a stronger army.

Africa, the Great Continent

Africa has been slow to develop economically, politically, and industrially. But it is a continent of free nations now. So Africa is taking a place of greater importance in the world. It is the second largest continent on earth. Africa alone is as large as the United States, Europe, and China put together.

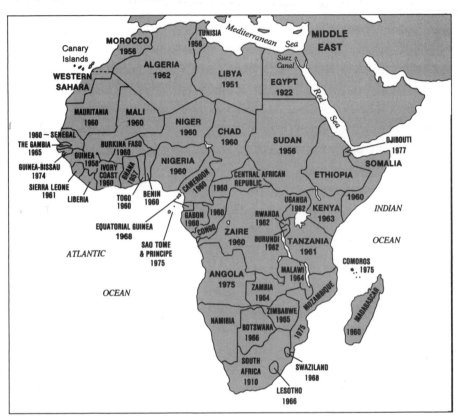

African nations become independent

Fewer than 100 years ago, Africa was called the Dark Continent, an unexplored land of mystery. Later it became a land to be owned, and it was divided up among stronger countries. Then World War II ended the days of European-ruled colonies in Africa. Today free African nations are growing stronger.

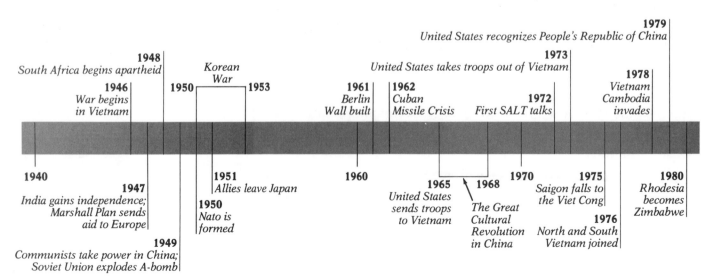

1979
United States recognizes People's Republic of China

1973
United States takes troops out of Vietnam

1948
South Africa begins apartheid

1950

Korean War

1953

1961
Berlin Wall built

1962
Cuban Missile Crisis

1972
First SALT talks

1978
Vietnam Cambodia invades

1946
War begins in Vietnam

1940

1947
India gains independence; Marshall Plan sends aid to Europe

1951
Allies leave Japan

1950
Nato is formed

1960

1965
United States sends troops to Vietnam

1968
The Great Cultural Revolution in China

1970

1975
Saigon falls to the Viet Cong

1976
North and South Vietnam joined

1980
Rhodesia becomes Zimbabwe

1949
Communists take power in China; Soviet Union explodes A-bomb

Points to Remember

◆ The Marshall Plan gave aid to war-torn Europe.

◆ After World War II, Germany was divided into a democratic West Germany and a communist-controlled East Germany.

◆ The United States and the Soviet Union were allies during the world wars. But after World War II, a cold war began between them.

◆ The Soviet Union has communist satellites in Eastern Europe, and it encourages the spread of communism throughout the world.

◆ The world powers hold peace talks to try to limit the buildup of nuclear arms.

◆ India gained its independence from Britain in 1947 and was divided into India and Pakistan. Both nations face overcrowding and food shortages.

◆ In 1949 the Communists took over China, forming the People's Republic of China. Nationalist Chinese set up their own government in Taiwan.

◆ The Allies occupied Japan after World War II. They helped set up a new, nonmilitaristic government there.

◆ The United States tried to help fight communism in Korea and in Vietnam. In Vietnam, the effort failed, and Vietnam became a communist-run country.

◆ African nations have gained independence from European imperialism since World War II.

Think About It!

1. How were France, Italy, East Germany, and West Germany governed after World War II?

2. What happened to European colonies after World War II?

3. Once a colony becomes an independent nation, what problems is it likely to face?

4. What trouble spots in the world have threatened to turn the cold war into a world war? What are some possible problem areas today?

5. What happened to the countries of Eastern Europe after World War II?

6. What efforts have been made to protect the world against a nuclear war?

7. Describe relations between the United States and the Soviet Union today.

8. Describe relations between the United States and the People's Republic of China today.

9. What happened back in the United States after U.S. troops were sent to Vietnam?

10. What is apartheid?

11. What happened to white minority rule in Rhodesia?

Chapter 15

The Middle East Today

Words to Know

hostages people held prisoner by an enemy until certain demands are met

hostile unfriendly, showing hate or dislike

terrorist a fighter who hopes to achieve certain goals by using force and random violence to frighten people

traitor one who betrays a cause, a friend, or a nation

Zionism the movement to set up a Jewish nation in Palestine

Look for the answers as you read:

1. Why did Jews consider Palestine their homeland?

2. Why did Arabs think that Palestine should be theirs?

3. How was the state of Israel formed?

4. Why did Palestinians end up in refugee camps?

5. What were the results of Anwar Sadat's visit to Israel in 1977?

6. What is OPEC, and what does it do?

7. What conflicts continue in the Middle East today?

People of the Middle East were often ruled by other lands. For hundreds of years, the Middle East had been part of the Ottoman Empire. After World War I, most of the Middle East fell under British control. Egypt, however, gained its independence from Britain in 1922. Meanwhile, France took control of Syria and Lebanon.

World War II weakened the European countries. This left the door open for Arab nationalists to gain independence for their countries. Most importantly, Arabs took control of their own oil fields. Oil deposits had been discovered in Iraq in 1927 and in Saudi Arabia in 1938. More huge oil fields were later found along the Persian Gulf. European and American oil companies had moved in to control the oil fields. The Middle Eastern nations saw little of their own oil wealth. But after World War II, many Arab nations gained tremendous riches and power because of their oil.

Nationalism in the Middle East

The Middle East today

In ancient days the Jews considered Palestine their homeland. They called it a land promised to them by God. They built a temple in Jerusalem, the holy city.

But almost 2,000 years ago, the Romans drove the Jews out of Jerusalem. Some Jews settled in an area of Palestine called Galilee. But most of the Jews fled from Palestine. They scattered around the world.

A Jewish Homeland in Palestine

Many Jews never gave up their dream of the promised homeland. In the late 1800s, Jews in Eastern Europe were persecuted. Some Jews started a movement called **Zionism**. Their goal was to make Palestine an independent Jewish nation. Jews from Europe began to settle in Palestine, which at that time was ruled by the Ottoman Turks.

By 1914 about 85,000 Jews had returned there. After World War I, Britain promised to create a Jewish homeland in Palestine. Meanwhile, the Arab population of Palestine had been increasing, too. And the Arabs living there did not like the strangers in their land.

After World War II, Zionism became more popular. Jews who had felt Hitler's persecution were ready for a homeland of their own. Many came to Palestine.

The State of Israel

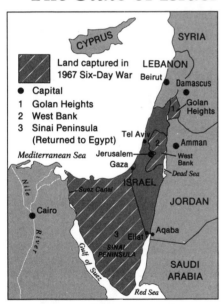

Israel and its neighbors.

In 1947 the United Nations voted to end British rule over Palestine. The United Nations knew there was a conflict between Arabs and Jews in Palestine. Arabs said that the land had been theirs for 2,000 years. Jews said that it had been theirs even before the Arabs had settled there. So the United Nations divided Palestine into two parts. One part was for Jews and the other for Arabs. The Jews agreed to the U.N. plan. But the Arabs were angry. They wanted all of Palestine to be an Arab state.

On May 14, 1948, David Ben-Gurion, the Zionist leader in Palestine, read a declaration of independence. He declared that the Jewish part of Palestine was the new state of Israel.

Israel was recognized immediately by the United States and then by the Soviet Union. The Arabs, however, declared war on Israel. On May 15, 1948, Israel was invaded by armies from the Arab nations of Syria, Egypt, Lebanon, Iraq, and Jordan.

Refugees of War

The Israelis were greatly outnumbered. And they had a shortage of weapons. But Israel won the war by the end of 1948. The state of Israel was firmly established. The lands left to the Arabs became part of Jordan.

About 700,000 Arabs fled Israel, becoming refugees. The homeless Palestinian Arabs lived in crowded refugee camps outside of Israel. Many live there still. These Palestinian refugees believe that their homes were stolen. Some of them formed a group of fighters called the Palestine Liberation Organization (PLO). Their goal is to win back their land.

After the war in 1948, about 700,000 Jews living in Arab nations were forced to leave. Jews left Iraq, Libya, and other countries. Most went to live in Israel.

Israel had won the 1948 war. But the problems of the Middle East were far from settled.

Middle East Tensions

Soon the superpowers became involved in the Israeli-Arab conflict. In 1955 the Soviets offered to sell arms to Egypt. This was followed by a conflict over the Suez Canal.

In 1956 Egypt took over the canal from Britain and France. Britain, France, and Israel then attacked Egypt. The United Nations arranged a cease-fire. The Suez Canal was held by Egypt. But the Arabs became even more **hostile** toward Israel.

The Six-Day War

In June of 1967, another war began. Israel fought the Arab nations of Egypt, Jordan, and Syria. In the first few minutes of the war, Israeli planes attacked the Arab airfields. Almost all of the Arab airplanes were destroyed on the ground. Then the Israeli army pushed through the Sinai Peninsula all the way to the Suez Canal. The war was over in six days! Israel occupied all of the Sinai Peninsula, Gaza Strip, and the West Bank. The West Bank was the section of Palestine that had become part of Jordan. And Israel also took control of East Jerusalem.

Israeli soldiers in the Negev Desert, Israel, 1967

The Yom Kippur War

Arab nations grew angrier. In 1973 Egypt, Syria, Jordan, and Iraq launched a surprise attack on Israel. It was called the Yom Kippur War. This was because the Arabs attacked on the Jewish holy day called Yom Kippur. This time, the Arabs almost won. Israel managed to defend itself. But it paid a high price in the number of lives lost.

Israeli border police, Bethlehem, Israeli-occupied West Bank

A Peace Treaty

In 1977 Egypt's president Anwar el-Sadat visited Israel. His visit surprised the world. It was the first move toward peace with Israel that any Arab leader had ever made. Then U.S. president Jimmy Carter invited Sadat and Israel's prime minister Menachem Begin to the United States. There the three leaders held discussions on how to end the Arab-Israeli conflict. These meetings led to the signing of the Camp David Accords in 1979. Israel promised to return all of the Sinai Peninsula to Egypt in exchange for peace. Israel also promised to allow the Palestinians in Gaza and on the West Bank to govern themselves. This part of the treaty has yet to be implemented.

Much of the world praised Sadat. In 1978 Sadat and Begin shared the Nobel Peace Prize. But many Arab nationalists were angry. They said that Sadat was a **traitor** to the Arab cause. In 1981 Sadat was assassinated by Moslem fanatics.

Anwar Sadat and Menachem Begin embracing after negotiating peace treaty, while President Jimmy Carter applauds

Middle East Conflicts Today

The fighting in the Middle East is not over. The Palestine Liberation Organization (PLO) still seeks a home for Palestinians. In 1970 the PLO was forced out of Jordan. In 1975 it became involved in civil war in Lebanon. The Palestinians still struggle with Israelis along borderlands, in Gaza, and on the West Bank. And the PLO has attracted world attention with **terrorist** attacks.

The Jews gained their homeland of Israel in Palestine, but the Palestinian Arabs lost their home. That conflict has yet to be solved.

Other Middle Eastern Conflicts: Lebanon, Iran, and Iraq

Today the people of the Middle East live in the shadow of war. While Palestinian terrorists strike out in a battle for a home, fighting in Lebanon goes on. In 1982 Israel had invaded Lebanon, seeking to destroy PLO bases. The PLO were forced to leave Lebanon. But once the Israeli army withdrew from Lebanon, the PLO came back.

*Destruction caused
by Israeli air raid,
Beirut, Lebanon*

Lebanon's civil war is partly based on religion. Moslems battle Christians for power. And different Moslem groups battle each other. In 1983 the United States became involved in the war. U.S. troops entered Lebanon as peace-keepers. The troops were taken out of Lebanon only after many U.S. marines were killed by Moslem terrorists.

The civil war has all but destroyed Lebanon, leaving its cities in shambles. Beirut, the capital of Lebanon, had been known as the "Paris" of the Middle East. Now much of it lies in ruins.

The country of Iran has seen conflict, too. Iranians were unhappy with their leader, the Shah. The Shah had a vicious secret police who made sure that he kept power.

In 1979, a 76-year old Moslem leader, the Ayatollah Khomeini, returned to Iran from exile in France. Khomeini led a successful revolution against the Shah. He then set up a Moslem republic following strict Islamic rules. Khomeini's followers wanted the Shah to stand trial for crimes they said he had committed. But the Shah had fled the country. Then in November 1979, Iranians captured the American embassy in Teheran, Iran's capital. They took American **hostages**, and they demanded the Shah's return.

Much of the world was angered by the Iranian action. But Iran would not give up the hostages. The Shah died in Egypt in July 1980. And in January 1981 the American hostages were finally freed.

Meanwhile, in 1980, Iran was attacked by its neighbor, Iraq. There had been bitter disputes over territory. Iraq hoped to win a quick victory over Iran. Saddam Hussain, leader of Iraq, thought that Iran had been weakened by the Islamic revolution. But neither Moslem nation could beat the other. The war dragged on for many years.

*Demonstrators demanding that
American hostages be put on trial,
Teheran, Iran*

There were huge land battles. Then both sides began firing missiles at each other's cities. And each country began to attack oil tankers in the Persian Gulf. In 1987 the U.S. sent its navy to the Gulf to protect the flow of oil.

Finally, in 1988, the United Nations was able to arrange a cease-fire between Iran and Iraq. Both countries had suffered such huge losses that they were willing to begin talking about ending the war.

Much of the Middle East has oil. All nations need oil, and world supplies are limited. Their oil fields give the Arab countries power.

An organization called OPEC (Organization of Petroleum Exporting Countries) manages that power. OPEC members include the oil-producing nations of the Middle East and the Latin American country of Venezuela.

Oil Power

An oil industry worker in the Middle East

OPEC sets the price of oil. OPEC can force up oil prices or withhold oil from certain countries. This gives OPEC tremendous power. During the Arab-Israeli wars of 1967 and 1973, the Arabs used their oil as a weapon. They cut off the flow of oil to the West. In 1973 this resulted in a severe oil shortage in the United States. Drivers were forced to wait in long lines at the gas pumps. And they had to pay a much higher price for each gallon they bought.

Some people in the Middle East are very, very wealthy because of oil. But the oil wealth remains in the hands of a few. Much of the profits from oil sales go toward building a strong Arab military.

Life in the Middle East

Residents of a kibbutz washing dishes, Nahal Snir, Israel

The Middle East is, without a doubt, a land of war and conflict. It faces serious problems that will have to be dealt with. Still, the Middle East has fine, modern cities, well-educated people, fertile farmlands, and productive industries.

One of the most industrialized and advanced nations of the Middle East is Israel. About 85 percent of Israel's people live and work in modern cities. Israel's farms are a source of pride. Most of Israel's land is poor. Some of the land is too rocky or steep for farming. Other areas get little rainfall. Only through hard work and agricultural know-how could those lands be productive. Still, Israel produces most of its own food.

Huge irrigation systems pump in water through underground pipelines. Scientists experiment with turning salt water from the Mediterranean and Red seas into fresh water to soak their fields.

The Israelis have not won the most perfect of lands. But they have worked hard to build their nation.

People of the Middle East: Yesterday and Today

Long before the birth of Christ, the first civilizations were forming along the Tigris and Euphrates rivers and along the Nile River. Those early people concerned themselves with producing food and irrigating their dry lands. They battled invaders who would take their lands. They argued over how they would worship their gods. In some ways, those people had much in common with today's Middle Eastern people.

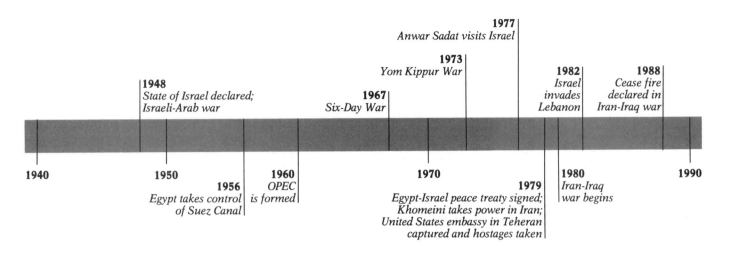

Points to Remember

◆ Most Middle Eastern nations gained independence from Britain and France after World War II.

◆ Zionists wanted to set up a Jewish state in Palestine.

◆ The United Nations divided Palestine between Arabs and Jews.

◆ In 1948 the Jews set up the state of Israel. The remaining lands of Palestine became part of the Arab state of Jordan.

◆ Since 1948 Arabs and Israelis have fought wars for control of those lands.

◆ Many Palestinians who had fled from Israel were left homeless. They were forced to live in crowded refugee camps. They formed the PLO and demanded their lands back.

◆ Many Arab nations have wealth and power because there is oil on their lands.

◆ The constant threat of war is a major problem in the Middle East today.

Think About It!

1. Why do both Jews and Arabs feel they have a claim to the land once called Palestine?

2. Both young men and young women are drafted into Israel's military. Why do you think that is done?

3. Why does OPEC have so much power in today's world?

4. How could trouble in the Middle East affect Soviet-U.S. cold war tensions?

Chapter 16

The World Today

Words to Know

astronaut   a person trained to make space flights

cosmonaut   Russian word meaning *astronaut*

nonrenewable   not replaceable once it's used up

radioactive fallout   deadly particles given off by a nuclear explosion

satellite   an object put into orbit around the earth

technology   science put to use in practical work

Look for the answers as you read:

1. Why is the late twentieth century sometimes called the Nuclear Age?

2. What are some of the uses of nuclear power?

3. Why is the late twentieth century sometimes called the Space Age?

4. How do advances in communication and transportation make the world seem smaller?

5. What is meant by a "developed" nation?

6. What is meant by a "third world" nation?

7. How have the roles of women changed?

8. What are some similarities between ancient peoples and people of today?

New York City skyscrapers

People call these times the "Nuclear Age" or the "Space Age" or the "Computer Age." Today's world is full of brand new inventions and discoveries. There are things now that Alexander the Great, Julius Caesar, Napoleon Bonaparte, or even dreamers like Leonardo da Vinci could never imagine. And yet in spite of all the progress, people today still have much in common with their ancestors.

The last half of the twentieth century is sometimes called the Nuclear Age. Actually, the idea of nuclear power began about 1905, with Albert Einstein. Einstein suggested that energy was contained in every atom. The first actual use of that energy came in 1945, when the United States exploded two atomic bombs over Japan. Those explosions ended World War II and began an age of development for atomic energy.

The Nuclear Age

Military Uses of Nuclear Power

The explosion of the first atomic bomb started the nations of the world on a race. It was a deadly race to build bigger weapons. Countries tried to outdo each other in the number and size of the bombs they built.

Now many nations have a weapon so destructive that the results of another world war are impossible to imagine. So, nations try to avoid that war. They meet and talk about peace. They discuss ways to limit the buildup of nuclear arms. The United States and the Soviet Union have held talks and signed treaties. And they hope to reach further agreements—perhaps even to get rid of nuclear weapons altogether. As yet, however, no complete agreement has been reached. Nuclear weapons still threaten the safety of the whole world. It is a reality that today's people must live with.

Peaceful Uses of Nuclear Energy

Although it was first used in a bomb, nuclear power has peacetime uses, too. The most important use is as a source of energy.

All nations use oil, coal, and natural gas for energy. These are all **nonrenewable** energy sources. Once they are used up, they are gone. As the population grows, the demand for energy also grows. People worry that we will run out of those traditional sources of energy.

The energy created in the nucleus of the atom can be used to run factories, to heat homes, and to light cities. Today this energy is produced in nuclear power plants around the world. Nuclear power is expensive. But it can provide unlimited energy for thousands of years. The question is: Is it safe?

Three Mile Island nuclear power plant, Harrisburg, Pennsylvania

Nuclear power plants must have strict safety regulations. A nuclear accident could mean tragedy. If something goes wrong, millions of people could be exposed to **radioactive fallout**.

Accidents happen. One serious nuclear accident happened in the United States in 1979. At the Three Mile Island nuclear power plant in Pennsylvania, failing equipment and human mistakes caused a near meltdown. There were no tragic results, but the public was frightened. People became aware that a disaster could happen! Stricter safety rules were set up. But some people still wondered about the future of nuclear power. They worried that the risk was too great.

In 1986 the Soviet Union faced a more serious nuclear accident. This disaster happened in a power plant in Chernobyl. Twenty-three people died, and the town of Chernobyl was evacuated. A radiation cloud moved from Chernobyl across several European nations. Traces of radiation were found in animals, in milk, and in plant life far from the actual accident site. No one is sure just what the long-range effects of such radiation might be.

Many people protest the building of nuclear power plants. They say that no amount of energy is worth the risk of nuclear disaster. Others maintain that nuclear power is a safe answer to the world's energy crisis. They point out that many people haved died in coal mine accidents over the years. Compared to this, only a few have died in accidents related to nuclear power plants. Those in favor of nuclear power also point out that it is clean. It causes much less pollution than coal or oil. But those against nuclear power have one very solid argument for their point of view. No safe method has as yet been discovered for disposing of nuclear waste.

The Space Age

Sometimes the last half of the twentieth century is called the Space Age. The Space Age began in 1957 when the Soviet Union launched the first man-made **satellite**. The satellite was called *Sputnik I.* Soon after, the United States launched its first satellite, *Explorer I.* The space race had begun.

In 1961 the Russians put the first human being into space. He was **cosmonaut** Yuri Gagarin. Then in 1969, U.S. **astronaut** Neil Armstrong became the first person to walk on the moon. Six hundred million people around the world watched this event on TV.

The first woman went into space in 1963. She was the Soviet cosmonaut Valentina V. Tereshkova. In 1983 the United States sent its first woman astronaut, Sally Ride, into space aboard the shuttle *Challenger.*

Space is another area where the United States and the Soviet Union race to be the best. But space can also be an arena for peace. In July 1975, three American astronants and two Russian cosmonauts met in space. As planned, their two spaceships hooked up. Then the Americans and Russians shook hands, shared a meal, and held a news conference for the world to see. They also conducted joint scientific experiments for two days.

The Space Age has only just begun. Many people expect that before too long, we will have colonies on the Moon. And people from Earth may someday live on Mars and on other planets. Unmanned spaceships have already landed on Mars and Venus and sent back pictures. Other ships have flown close to Jupiter and Saturn. Perhaps someday, we may even go to the stars!

The exploration of space is exciting. But it is also difficult, expensive, and dangerous. In January 1986, the space shuttle *Challenger* exploded shortly after takeoff. All the people on board were killed. And there have been other accidents in which people have died. But many people feel that the rewards from space exploration are worth the risks.

The space shuttle Challenger *several days before the disaster*

*An office secretary
using a word processor,
a specialized type of computer*

The Computer Age

Computers are electronic machines. They solve problems and answer questions. They store information. Computers are used around the world to help people make better use of their time.

Computers have been improved steadily since World War II. At first they were very large, very expensive, and difficult to run. Now they are much smaller and are used by millions of people. A computer that once filled an entire room now fits into a package the size of a breadbox!

At first people worried that computers would replace humans in many jobs. And in some cases this has happened. But computers have created many more new jobs. Computers give people the time and freedom to get more work done.

The Shrinking World

Developments in transportation and communication have made the world seem smaller. People in one part of the world now know what is happening elsewhere.

Television has changed twentieth-century life as much as any other one invention. So many Americans protested involvement in the Vietnam War because television cameras brought the action to them. They saw for themselves the suffering of American soldiers and Vietnamese villagers.

Television news takes the Israeli-Arab conflicts into millions of homes. People of the world see the injustices of apartheid in South Africa and hunger in Ethiopia with their own eyes.

Also, hundreds of communications satellites circle the earth. They beam radio, television, telephone, and computer signals around the world. Satellites in space can take weather pictures to make forecasts anywhere in the world.

New methods of travel have also made a difference. First the railroad, then automobiles, and then airplanes made the world seem smaller. With modern jet planes, a trip across oceans and continents is an easy matter.

As the world seems to grow smaller, nations have a greater influence on each other. Trade has long affected cultures and civilizations. Ideas have always spread and mingled as trade increased. Now it is routine for nations to trade their goods and their ideas worldwide.

Developed Nations and Third World Nations

Some nations in the world are called "developed" nations. They have many industries. They import and export products. Most people who live in developed nations have a fairly high standard of living. They can read and write. They benefit from the advances of modern science and **technology**. The United States, the Soviet Union, Canada, France, Great Britain, Japan, and West Germany are just some of the developed nations.

Many countries are less developed. They are sometimes called "developing" or "third world" nations. The name "third world" comes from the idea that the West developed first, the East developed second, and now the third world is developing.

Many people in these developing nations are poor. Large numbers live by farming the land. But their methods of agriculture are often outdated. There are few industries in developing nations. Their standard of living is lower, and a large number of the population cannot read or write.

India, Afghanistan, and Mexico are examples of less developed countries. Many South American and African nations are developing countries. Some of the less developed nations, like Nigeria and Venezuela, have rich oil deposits.

The third world countries are more dependent on other nations. Their economies can be easily upset by weather, by a year of bad farm crops, or by a war. Sometimes the more developed countries help the third world nations by lending them money or sending supplies. The more advanced nations also send people to teach modern farming methods, health care, and engineering.

Just Imagine . . . a Trip Forward in Time

Picture the days of ancient Greece. Imagine a Greek athlete running an Olympic race. It is 700 B.C. The young man pulls ahead of the other racers on a dusty road. He gasps the warm air. His lungs ache with the effort. As he crosses the finish line, he closes his eyes and raises his arms over his head in victory.

When he opens his eyes again, he expects to find himself surrounded by cheering Greeks. He can almost feel the crown of olive leaves about to be placed on his head.

Instead . . . the racer finds himself in a crowded, modern stadium. It is 1984, Los Angeles, California, the 23d Summer Olympics. People are cheering, but they are not all Greeks. They are people from around the whole world. And no olive leaves await the racer. Instead he is awarded a shiny, gold medal. Somehow our racer has been jolted forward in time more than 2,000 years to the 1980s.

What will he find? What undreamed of wonders will our racer discover?

He will find a whole new world of medicine. Doctors can actually replace worn out or diseased body parts. Sometimes those replacements come from people who have died. Other times the parts are man-made. The young Greek time-traveler can hardly believe it. These modern doctors can even replace a person's heart!

People treat each other in a different way now. The Greek racer is surprised to find himself surrounded by women athletes. Women, he will discover, have a whole new role in society. In many places they are treated as equals with men. They work side by side with men in all kinds of jobs. Women have become leaders in science, in space travel, in medicine, and in business.

And where are the slaves? At last, most societies realize that all people deserve the same respect and the same chances. They deserve an education, job opportunities, and a fair chance at making a good life. People move more easily from one social class to another now.

Spaceships to the moon, automobiles that speed people to their destinations, airplanes, television, telephones . . . the list of new wonders is endless.

Dr. Robert Jarvik and the artificial heart he designed

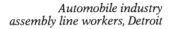
*Automobile industry
assembly line workers, Detroit*

Has anything remained the same? Most people still live in family groups, although many of those groups are smaller. People still have the same basic needs for food and shelter. And people still have trouble getting along. There are still those who want to be conquerors and who seek power at all costs. There are still those who must struggle to hold on to their cultures and their homes. Different peoples still do not know and understand each other well enough. And people still fear what they do not understand.

Human beings are still curious, too. They still need to learn, to explore, and to discover. There will always be some questions to answer: What lies beyond the sun? Are there worlds and peoples other than our own? And can the inhabitants of this world ever live together completely at peace?

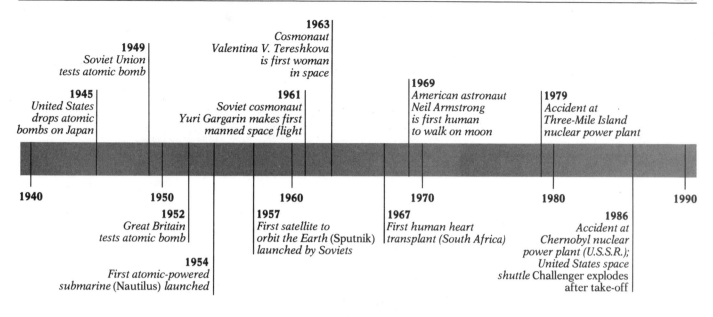

1945
United States drops atomic bombs on Japan

1949
Soviet Union tests atomic bomb

1963
Cosmonaut Valentina V. Tereshkova is first woman in space

1961
Soviet cosmonaut Yuri Gargarin makes first manned space flight

1969
American astronaut Neil Armstrong is first human to walk on moon

1979
Accident at Three-Mile Island nuclear power plant

1940   1950   1960   1970   1980   1990

1952
Great Britain tests atomic bomb

1957
First satellite to orbit the Earth (Sputnik) *launched by Soviets*

1967
First human heart transplant (South Africa)

1986
Accident at Chernobyl nuclear power plant (U.S.S.R.); United States space shuttle Challenger *explodes after take-off*

1954
First atomic-powered submarine (Nautilus) *launched*

Points to Remember

◆ Nuclear power is used for weapons and as a source of energy in peacetime.

◆ People worry about the dangers of an accident in a nuclear power plant and about the safe disposal of nuclear waste.

◆ Television makes people more aware and concerned about what is going on around the world.

◆ Developed nations have advanced technology, a higher standard of living, and strong trade programs.

◆ Third world nations are less developed, poorer, and more dependent on other countries.

◆ There is more opportunity for movement between social classes in today's world.

◆ Many things have changed, but people still have to deal with problems of ignorance, prejudice, persecution, and war.

Think About It!

1. What do you consider some of the most startling developments in science in the last ten years?

2. How did the invention of television make the world seem smaller?

3. What are space satellites used for?

4. How have human rights and ideas of equality changed?

5. In some societies older people were highly honored and respected for their wisdom and experience. How are older people treated in today's society?

6. What do you consider some of the greatest challenges today's world has to face?